WAS IT NOT I?

WAS IT NOT I?

And Other Questions God Asks

W. E. McCUMBER

Beacon Hill Press of Kansas City
Kansas City, Missouri

PREFACE

One of God's questions in the Old Testament attracted me to all of God's questions there. I examined them one by one in my personal devotions for several months. Each morning I responded to them in writing.

I heard them; I did not merely overhear them. They were more than ancient words frozen in history. They became personal address. God confronted me with them and compelled response to them. I learned more about Him, about His Word, and about myself. I became a better person and an abler servant for having studied them.

That God speaks to us is an expression of His grace. That He questions us defines our accountability. We must answer Him.

These devotional reflections are suggestive, not exhaustive. They are not analyses, not learned discussions, not the stuff of commentaries. I hope they will provoke further study and response from those who read them. They are brief, for I am given to brevity.

Some of them led to sermons. This is not surprising, for all that nourishes my soul becomes part of the soul-feeding I do as a preacher. Perhaps preachers who read them will find them a seedbed for sermons also. However, their first aim is devotional—direct, biblical, and challenging at those spiritual levels where we all most truly live.

PREFACE

1

Where are you?

(Gen. 3:9)

Scripture reading: Gen. 3:1-24

God's questions, recorded in the Bible, supply an excellent framework for a study in relational theology.

His first question was addressed to Adam, after sin had intruded upon human consciousness.

"Where are you?" God wasn't seeking information. No forest can hide a guilty man from the all-seeing God. He knew where Adam was and asked the question because Adam needed to know where he was. The sinner needed to face the truth about his broken relationships to God, to his wife, and to the place in which they lived. Sin never leaves identities, relations, and securities unaltered.

So the question was posed by the all-knowing God to the unknowing man. And it was asked, not to condemn him, for sin brings its own condemnation, but to announce a way back to God, a plan to restore broken relationships.

"Where are you?" In relation to God, to others, to the earth, where are you? Each of us needs to hear and answer that question every day.

2

Who told you that you were naked?

(Gen. 3:11)

Scripture reading: Gen. 2:15—3:12

*B*efore they sinned, man and woman were naked and not ashamed (2:25). Clothed with the light and glory of innocence, of a right and happy relationship to Creator and creation, they had no reason to feel shame.

Having sinned, they were guilty, afraid, disoriented, threatened, unhappy—and therefore ashamed.

No one told them they were naked. No one had to tell them. Sin is self-verifying. It produces negative effects, eloquent of misery, grief, and pain.

Sin strips men and women of all that is good, of all that makes them comfortable in the presence of God. Sin strips mankind of dignity, integrity, liberty, and security. It reduces people to a nakedness that threatens to become nothingness.

And a person knows that without being told.

3

Have you eaten from the tree that I commanded you not to eat from?

(Gen. 3:11)

Scripture reading: Gen. 3:1-12

The question is not designed to elicit information but to encourage confession. There can be no deliverance from sin until a person takes responsibility for his actions, until he *owns* his sin.

Alas, Adam could not bring himself to say, "I have sinned." Instead, he blamed his wife—and by a none-too-subtle implication he tried to blame God: "The woman *you* put here with me" (v. 12, italics added).

A sinner's first instinct is to blame someone or something else. We try to finger our parents, our spouses, our society, our heredity, our environment—anyone and anything but ourselves.

God did not buy Adam's excuse, and He doesn't buy ours. We will never find pardon and peace until we say "I"—not "him" or "her" or "you" or "they" or "it," but *I*.

4

What is this you have done?

(Gen. 3:13)

Scripture reading: Gen. 3:1-16

*T*he question is directed to Eve. Adam could not escape his guilt by blaming her, but she too had sinned and must face her own record of wrongdoing.

She answered, "The serpent . . ." The deceiver was no excuse for her transgression. When God has spoken His clear no, we cannot blame a rebellious yes on the devil or on our kinfolks.

Ignorance did not make the deception possible. The will of God had been stated without ambiguity. Eve sinned against light, not against darkness.

Sin is not the issue of ignorance, as certain famous philosophers have taught. Sin is the issue of rebellion, as the Bible makes plain.

Education—even "higher education"—is not the answer to sin. Education cannot save; it barely civilizes. Education does not make one a saint; it makes him a more clever and sophisticated sinner.

Atonement is necessary to remove the guilt and power of sin, and only God as Man could provide that Atonement.

5

Why are you angry?

(Gen. 4:6)

Scripture reading: Gen. 4:1-15

God accepted Abel's offering but disregarded Cain's. Exactly why Cain's offering was rejected, we are not told. Many explanations have been offered, but no agreement has been reached among scholars.

This much can be said: The expanded question makes it clear that *Cain knew why.* "Why is your face downcast? If you do what is right, will you not be accepted?" (vv. 6-7).

There was the rub! Cain wanted acceptance with God on his own terms. The sinner insists on playing God. Instead of listening and obeying when God reveals the way out of sin, man's pride compels him to attempt his own salvation. His arrogance only served to worsen sin, to increase guilt, and to further offend God.

Like a crouching lion, sin waits to devour the man who tries to dictate terms of acceptance to God (v. 7). God cannot be manipulated and controlled by human rituals. God will be God, and angry, pouting sinners cannot usurp His authority, though they do try.

6

Where is your brother . . . ?

(Gen. 4:9)

Scripture reading: Gen. 4:1-15

A man must answer for himself: "Where are you?" He must also answer for others: **"Where is your brother . . . ?"** Life is not a game of solitaire. Each person is involved with all persons. To be human is to be persons in relationship, not in isolation.

Jesus insisted that love for God must be wedded to love for neighbors to form the substance of the whole law. The Bible insists that no man lives or dies unto himself. Paul taught that Christians are members of one another in the Church, the Body of Christ.

"Am I my brother's keeper?" snarled Cain (v. 9). No, we are our brothers' brother. "Abel kept flocks" (v. 2). The murderous Cain slaughtered him as he would have killed an animal. He treated Abel like one of the flock, not like a brother.

Cain could not escape his crime or regain his peace. Earth cannot be home when a brother has been slain. Cain became a vagabond.

Adam broke with God; Cain broke with Abel. Horizontal relationships cannot be sustained when the vertical relationship has been sundered. "Where are you?" "Where is your brother?" Ultimately the questions and answers merge into one.

7

Is anything too hard for the Lord?

(Gen. 18:14)

Scripture reading: Gen. 18:1-15

*S*arah laughed when promised a son after she was "past the age of childbearing" (v. 11). God challenged her with His question, **"Is anything too hard for the Lord?"** and repeated His promise.

Suddenly afraid, Sarah added lying to laughter. She denied her original response. It is never far from doubt to denial.

God's word is self-authenticating, self-fulfilling. Laughter and lying aside, Sarah did conceive and birthed a son at the age of 90.

Abraham named him Isaac, meaning "he laughs" (21:3). Sarah, who laughed in disbelief, now laughed in delight. God's covenant child had arrived. God's promise had been fulfilled. Death had yielded to life.

Every living Jew is descended from Isaac. Every living Jew is proof, therefore, that nothing is too hard for the Lord. History is no laughing matter.

8

Shall I hide from Abraham what I am about to do?

(Gen. 18:17)

Scripture reading: Gen. 18:16-33

God was about to bring a devastating judgment upon Sodom and Gomorrah, ancient cities notorious for evil.

Why tell Abraham? Because he was the "friend of God" and had relatives in Sodom who were endangered by the threatened destruction.

Abraham, in a moving passage, is heard pleading that righteous persons might not perish with the wicked. Before Abraham ended his plea, God agreed to spare the cities if 10 righteous persons could be found in them.

They were not found, but when the cities were destroyed, Abraham's relatives escaped through the merciful intervention of angels.

God has not hidden from any Bible reader His intention to bring an awful final judgment upon sinful mankind. Our unsaved loved ones are at risk, unprepared to meet the coming Judge in peace. Does this not summon us to intercede for them? We are to tell God about them and to tell them about Him. That intercession and witness is His way of gaining entrance to their lives.

9

What is your name?

(Gen. 32:27)

Scripture reading: Gen. 32:1-32

*T*he "man" with whom Jacob wrestled was God. God's question was not a request for an identification card. It challenged Jacob to admit that he had lived up—or down—to his name, which meant a usurper of others.

After stating his name, a way of admitting his sins, Jacob was given a new name to mark a new heart and a new life. He became "Israel."

God will not change us until we confess our need to be changed. Until we honestly face up to who we are and what we have done, we deprive ourselves of the grace that can make us new persons. God saves the unworthy but not the *unwilling* from their sins.

When once-greedy and once-grasping Jacob meets his brother, he urges a large gift upon him, saying, "I have all I need" (33:11). That statement indicates a great change in Jacob. He is proof that new names and new lives are possible through the grace of God as Man—Jesus Christ.

10

What is that in your hand?

(Exod. 4:2)

Scripture reading: Exod. 3:1—4:17

*M*oses held a staff, an instrument common to shepherds. Cast down, it became a serpent; taken up, it remained a staff. What we possess may be a tool for God or a threat to us, depending upon our obedience or disobedience to God's assignments.

Our money, our talents, our material possessions, our educational advantages, our social influences—every resource great or small—can honor God or ruin us. The gifts are His; the choices are ours.

Withheld from God, our assets menace us. Employed for Him, they fortify us. Serpents or staffs—it's all determined by our assent or refusal to serve His purpose.

With that staff Moses worked miracles as the leader of God's redeemed people. Common instruments are a power for liberation when God has His way.

You may not have much in your hand, but how much it can mean depends upon whether or not you commit it to God.

11

Who gave man his mouth?

(Exod. 4:11)

Scripture reading: Exod. 4:1-17

Moses tries to duck the summons to lead Israel out of Egypt, pleading a slow tongue. He gets a quick response: **"Who gave man his mouth?** Who makes him deaf or mute? Who gives him sight or makes him blind? Is it not I, the Lord? Now go; I will help you speak and will teach you what to say" (vv. 11-12).

God calls a limited person but promises unlimited help. Our infirmities do not excuse us from His assignments, for whom He calls He also instructs and enables. "I will help." "I . . . will teach." That is enough to silence our objections and enlist our service.

God gives us our mouths, but He does not coerce our use of them. Serving God is a matter of choice. The consequences of our choice, however, are not options. The mouth yielded to Him is blessed and used. The mouth refused to Him is cursed, misused, and speaks finally the condemnation of the uncommitted.

It is better to be slow of speech for God than glib of tongue for oneself.

12

What about your brother, Aaron . . . ?

(Exod. 4:14)

Scripture reading: Exod. 4:14

*T*he question is asked in anger. God is weary of the excuses Moses keeps making. They all finally reduce to, "Please send someone else" (v. 13).

Aaron will become a spokesman for Moses. God accommodates himself to His servant's fears. But Moses will wish a thousand times that he had not forced the situation. Aaron's mouth will create more problems than solutions. It will speak more forcibly against Moses than for him. A stammering Moses and a lockjawed Aaron would have been a better arrangement.

Compromises and concessions are won from God to our detriment, not to our advantage. Moses was slow of speech, but Aaron was swift to rebel. His egoism would offset his eloquence. His mouth would have been better gagged than engaged.

Moses asked, "Who am I . . . ?" (3:11). He took stock of his lacks and limitations. He should have asked, "Whose am I?" He might then have escaped all the troubles Aaron caused or occasioned. God knows what He is doing!

13

Why are you crying out to me? Tell the Israelites to move on.

(Exod. 14:15)

Scripture reading: Exod. 14:1-31

*I*srael was between a rock and a hard place. The Sea of Reeds shimmered before them; the dust of a pursuing army darkened the air behind them. They growled at Moses, and he cried out to God. The answer was both rebuke and rescue. **"Why are you crying out to me? Tell the Israelites to move on."**

There is a time to pray and a time to march, a time to plead the promises and a time to act upon the promises. Prayer becomes complaint and unbelief when we refuse to venture upon the Word of God. It was into the sea and live, or stand on the shore and die! Forward at God's command or backward to Pharaoh's bondage.

Crying out for help brings God to the rescue. Crying out in fear and unbelief forfeits divine intervention. Nothing can substitute for the obedient execution of the expressed will of God, not even continued prayer.

The time comes when prayer must give place to a resolute "Amen" and a quickstep into the promised future. Feet, do your stuff!

14

How long will you refuse to keep my commands and my instructions?

(Exod. 16:28)

Scripture reading: Exod. 16:1-30

Manna from heaven fed an undeserving, grumbling people. They were not to receive it on the Sabbath, but some of them went looking for it anyhow, prompting God's angry question.

The question was flung at innocent Moses, not at the guilty culprits. Such is the price of leadership—the captain must answer for the crew. If discipline breaks down or mutiny occurs, he is accountable to higher authority. "You" supplants "they." Small wonder that Moses was so reluctant to assume the burdens of leadership.

God answers His own "How long . . . ?" He decides just when to bring judgment. If judgment awaited the consent of the guilty, it would be deferred forever. God, however, will not eternalize unpunished sin.

To lead is to bleed, and the wounds come as often from one's friends as from his foes. People need, want, even demand leadership, but they often are stubborn and rebellious when their selfish desires are ignored. And I'm talking about God's people. Ask Moses. Ask any pastor.

15

What else will he sleep in?

(Exod. 22:27)

Scripture reading: Exod. 22:25-27

God's reference is to the poor man who has pawned his cloak. The moneylender must return it by sunset, for it is both cloak and cover for the indigent person. Too poor to own more than the clothes on his back, such a man must huddle within his cloak or lack sufficient warmth to permit sleep.

God pities the poor and champions their cause. He waves no magic wand to eliminate poverty. The human problem must be humanely solved. That is our business. But God makes it His business to legislate and judge on behalf of earth's powerless and homeless poor.

Those who lend to them may look to God for interest. Those who give to them honor Him. Those who oppress them insult and anger Him.

God in Christ identifies with the one-cloak poor man who slept out of doors. Jesus said, "Foxes have holes and birds of the air have nests, but the Son of Man has no place to lay his head" (Luke 9:58). Compassionate treatment of the poor is one proof of genuine discipleship to Him.

16

Is the Lord's arm too short?

(Num. 11:23)

Scripture reading: Num. 11:4-34

*I*srael had bread but they wanted meat. Are we ever satisfied with God's gifts?

The Lord said, "You will get meat until you loathe it." Moses asked, "Where is all that meat coming from? Slaughter every animal in the herds, catch every fish in the sea, and we still won't have enough meat for this multitude."

God broke in with a question: **"Is the Lord's arm too short?** You will now see whether or not what I say will come true for you" (v. 23). Moses was counting cows and fish when he should have been measuring God's reach!

God dumped enough quail on the camp of Israel to exhaust every woman's recipes and bloat every man's belly. The people ate to their ruin. Severe plague broke out among them and filled a cemetery to which the name "Craving" was given.

They got what they wanted, what they demanded out of ingratitude, and it killed them. Isn't that human history in a nutshell?

17

Why . . . were you not afraid to speak against my servant Moses?

(Num. 12:8)

Scripture reading: Num. 12:1-15

*J*ealous of Moses, Aaron and Miriam challenged his authority and slandered his marriage. The Lord confronted the petty rebels in judgment.

Defending the fidelity of Moses, and declaring himself to be the source of Moses' authority, God afflicted Miriam with leprosy.

It is the Lord's prerogative to choose His spokesmen and leaders. It is His people's responsibility to listen to the word He sends by them. That responsibility even includes listening to their kinfolks!

Moses' brother and sister rejected his authority. Joseph's brothers scorned his God-given dreams. The brothers of Jesus regarded Him as mentally ill. The list could be extended by thousands. Nevertheless, God still refuses to submit His appointees for human confirmation.

Let the Lord speak and lead by whom He will! Let us find our joy in their ministry, not defying them but supporting them in love.

18

If her father had spit in her face,
would she not have been in disgrace
for seven days?

(Num. 12:14)

Scripture reading: Num. 12:1-15

*H*ow gracious and forgiving was Moses. When the
Lord smote Miriam with leprosy, her big-souled
brother prayed, "O God, please heal her!" (v. 13).

God is no less kind but much less soft. **"If her father
had spit in her face, would she not have been in disgrace
for seven days?"** Miriam's privileged position could not
exempt her from judgment. She was to be confined for a
week before being readmitted to the society whose unity
and peace she had been willing to sacrifice to her own ambition.

To oppose the Lord's servant is to oppose his Master.
No one is too highly favored by blood, money, or office to
escape the consequence of trying to veto God's actions.

The Lord who heard Miriam's wicked protest also
heard Moses' gracious prayer. He responded to both in
sovereign wisdom and love.

A greater than Moses would pray from the Cross, "Father, forgive them, for they do not know what they are doing" (Luke 23:34). Aren't we glad He did?

19

How long will these people treat me with contempt?

(Num. 14:11)

Scripture reading: Num. 14:1-25

*F*earful men, with what someone has called a "grass-hopper complex," refused to enter Canaan. They grumbled against Moses and threatened to return to Egypt.

God's glory appeared and silenced their babble of protest and fear. To Moses He said, **"How long will these people treat me with contempt?** How long will they refuse to believe in me, in spite of all the miraculous signs I have performed among them?"** (v. 11).

He proposed a radical answer to His own questions. He would wipe them out and call another nation from the loins of Moses.

Moses pled for their continued existence as a forgiven people. You are identified with them, he reminded God. If You annihilate them, Your name will be blasphemed among the heathen as a synonym for failure. In great love pardon them, the anxious leader begged.

For Moses' sake pardon was granted. For the sake of justice punishment was decreed. They would live but they would never enter Canaan. Their bones would bleach in the desert where 10 times over they had ignored God's miracles and disobeyed His commands. Once again the sovereign God determines the answer to His own question, "How long ... ?"

20

How long will this wicked community grumble against me?

(Num. 14:27)

Scripture reading: Num. 14:20-35

*T*hey would grumble as long as they lived, unfortunately! They would die as grumblers, occupy desert graves, and never see Canaan.

Their children would possess the Promised Land, with memories of parental failures to serve them as salutary warnings. But first the children would suffer 40 years of homeless wandering because of their parents' rebellion against God—a terrible price for an unhappy legacy.

Our grumbling against God is never a private matter. We are too involved with others to contain either blessings or judgments without spillover. Faith and doubt, with their consequences, are contagious. To live for God is to live for others as well. To sin against God is to sin against others also.

The present generation is more vocal about personal rights than social responsibilities. Doing "my own thing" is the first law of behavior for masses. That is the sure path to sorrow, not to happiness. Being truly human is a matter of relationships, not of isolation.

21

Who are these men with you?

(Num. 22:9)

Scripture reading: Num. 22:1-38

God knew who they were and what they wanted. The question was intended to alert Balaam to the kind of company he was keeping and to the consequences of traveling with that pack of wolves. Balaam could have spared himself a ton of misery had he listened to God when told, "Do not go with them" (v. 12).

They were men who sought to curse those whom God had chosen to bless. They made Balaam a handsome offer for his prophetic services, but no reward can compensate for opposing God. Titles and wealth are simply fodder to fatten beasts for slaughter when such honors are accepted at the price of offending the Almighty.

Balaam "loved the wages of wickedness" (2 Pet. 2:15), but he could collect them only by forfeiting the greater wealth of peace and power with God.

God has questions to ask about the company we keep. Who are they? Why are we with them? Our characters, habits, and destinies are in the answers.

22

Have I not commanded you?

(Josh. 1:9)

Scripture reading: Josh. 1:1-18

*J*oshua was a battle-proven soldier. He understood command. Ordered to lead Israel into Canaan, he had no options. The Supreme Commander's order could only be saluted and obeyed.

Strength and courage were commanded. That meant burdens and battles awaited. Meditation upon the Law and unswerving obedience to it were also commanded, for Joshua was leading a people who were covenant-bound to God.

Upon the awesome task confronting Joshua fell the enormous shadow of a titanic predecessor—Moses. How assuring it must have been to hear a promise added to the commands: "As I was with Moses, so I will be with you; I will never leave you nor forsake you" (v. 5). God enables what He commands.

"Have I not commanded you?" The "I" is rationale enough for the choice of the "you." The "I" is reinforcement enough for the "you." Whoever you are, you cannot fail when you march and fight at the command and with the promise of God.

23

What are you doing down on your face?

(Josh. 7:10)

Scripture reading: Josh. 7:1-26

*M*ighty Jericho fell but tiny Ai stood. Israel had been defeated. Behind the political disaster lay a moral reason. Achan's theft of spoil from Jericho had violated God's command and forfeited His presence.

Puzzled Joshua fell on his face to lament the defeat and to seek from God an explanation. He feared other and worse defeats as a consequence. Israel's future and God's honor were at risk. The situation was desperate.

"Stand up!" the Lord commanded. **"What are you doing down on your face?** Israel has sinned . . . stolen . . . lied"** (vv. 10-11). The Presence that assured victory would be withdrawn unless righteous judgment was executed at once.

Prayer is no substitute for obedience or repentance or judgment. Up on your feet, not down on your face! Those are stern orders that many spineless churches need to hear in a day when devotions flourish but discipline declines.

God demands obedience. He is not an elected official who exercises a delegated authority through the sufferance of the voters. He is God.

24

Am I not sending you?

(Judg. 6:14)

Scripture reading: Judg. 6:1-24

Someone had to deliver Israel from the oppressive Midianites. God tapped a fellow named Gideon for the awesome task. **"Am I not sending you?"**

Gideon was a farmer, not a fighter. His self-esteem was lower than a worm's instep. "I am the least in my family," he whined (v. 15).

God countered his doubt with a promise: "I will be with you" (v. 16). Talk about a big I and a little you! With the support of God, however, ordinary persons can achieve extraordinary victories.

God called him "mighty warrior" (v. 12). God sees us as we can be, not as we have been. The difference between what we are and what we can become is made by His presence and power, as we respond in faith.

Whoever God sends can go in courage and peace. A man cannot fail when God goes with him. The Sender is also the Goer, and that assures victory, whoever the sendee is. The least can do the most when God is in charge.

25

When . . . you cried to me for help, did I not save you . . . ?

(Judg. 10:11-12)

Scripture reading: Judg. 10:6-16

*A*gain and again the Lord had raised up judges to deliver oppressed Israel. Just as often they forgot His mercies and turned from Him to serve false gods. Once more harassed, they confess their sins and implore His help.

"When . . . you cried to me for help, did I not save you . . . ?" He had been patiently faithful to them, despite their wretched disloyalty. Now, He says, "I've had enough of your infidelity. Call on the idols you have served. Let them rescue you!" That's fair enough. It's just the answer that such ungrateful sinners deserved.

But mercy triumphs over justice. God's love exceeds His patience. "He could bear Israel's misery no longer" (v. 16) and summoned yet another deliverer for them.

Is that wonderful? Well, think of this. In time *He himself came* for us all. "God was reconciling the world to himself in Christ" (2 Cor. 5:19). Nothing is more amazing, more enduring, more liberating than God's love!

26

Why do you ask my name?
It is beyond understanding.

(Judg. 13:18)

Scripture reading: Judg. 13:1-24

M anoah's motive sounds good. He wanted to know God's name in order to use it in worship and praise. But no man can penetrate the mystery of God, and those who attempt it usually have ulterior motives. They seek to exploit Him.

God's name stands for who He is, and what He does, and the meaning of that being and doing for us.

His name is "wonderful" (RSV). It exceeds understanding. We cannot fully comprehend ourselves or one another. How much less can we grasp the whole truth of God's nature, purpose, and operations?

Our little opinions and criticisms of God would be comical were they not so frequently querulous, arrogant, and defiant.

We should rejoice in what we can understand of Him, and stand at the borders of knowledge in love, trust, and reverence. Instead, we too often pout because He doesn't fit our notions or grant our wishes.

With the mess we make of our own lives, how can any of us wish to do a makeover on God?

27

Why do you honor your sons more than me . . . ?

(1 Sam. 2:29)

Scripture reading: 1 Sam. 2:12-36

A man's first duty is to God, not to his family. Eli had been chosen for the priesthood, and the honor extended also to his sons. Where Eli had served honestly and lovingly, however, his sons had been contemptuous, selfish, wicked, and cruel, disgracing their office.

Eli rebuked them but failed to depose them. He should have honored God by imposing strict judgment upon them. His leniency served to enhance their contempt for the people and the law. Now God decides and declares their judgment. They will be killed, and a faithful priest will be raised up to succeed them.

We honor people best when we honor God first. We honor people best when we rebuke sin, demand repentance, promise forgiveness, and proclaim judgment. Love without truth is life without honor.

True love is tougher than affection. It so binds us to God that it frees us even from our families. We will not please them at the cost of displeasing Him.

28

How long will you mourn for Saul, since I have rejected him as king over Israel?

(1 Sam. 16:1)

Scripture reading: 1 Sam. 15:10—16:13

*S*amuel loved Saul. Samuel had anointed Saul to be Israel's first king. Saul's growing pride and waning faith had shattered the prophet's hopes and dreams. Pronouncing divine judgment upon the disobedient monarch became Samuel's doleful task. That done, the prophet was depressed.

The Lord is King over heaven and earth. Heaven has but one King, but earth can be supplied with any number of rulers. It was time to recognize the truth that the kingdom remained, though the king had been rejected. Undue mourning was a way of second-guessing God, of questioning His right to reject one ruler and to choose another.

God's question jarred Samuel from fruitless grief to positive action. He went to Bethlehem and anointed David to become Israel's next king. The secret mission affirmed that God rules and that the future is secured, not by any human dynasty, but by divine sovereignty.

Grief and mourning are natural and inevitable. But human emotions, however normal, must not become unspoken complaints about God's decisions and actions.

29

Are you the one to build me a house to dwell in?

(2 Sam. 7:5)

Scripture reading: 2 Sam. 7:1-17

*D*avid lived in a cedar palace. The ark of God was housed in a tent. The comparison was an embarrassment to David. He resolved to build a suitable dwelling for that priceless symbol of God's presence and glory in the midst of His people.

God vetoed the proposal. The son of David, instead, would become Israel's first Temple-builder. David's devotion would be expressed as a contributor and fund-raiser, but Solomon would claim the honor of building and dedicating the house of God.

"Man proposes but God disposes." That is His right. All our plans are subject to divine approval or disapproval. His wisdom is perfect, His decisions are final. There is no appeal from the divine yes or no. Our only options are obedience, with its consequent blessing, or disobedience, with its resultant curse.

Let God be God. Let men be content with being men. History proves that men make terrible gods!

30

Why did you despise the word of the Lord by doing what is evil in his eyes?

(2 Sam. 12:9)

Scripture reading: 2 Sam. 12:1-14

When God issues a law, no man is above it. From king to commoner, all must answer to Him. When men enforce the law, the commoner will be punished, but the king will be excused. God shows no such craven partiality.

"The sword will never depart from your house" (v. 10). Adultery and murder were David's sins, and these same evils plagued his family throughout their history. Sin's wages are paid in kind, and the coins are dropped into royal palms as surely as they are dropped into the hands of peasants.

God does not allow king or people to define evil. His eyes decide and His Word declares what is good and what is evil. No higher court can vacate His rulings, no royal culprit can escape His justice. To despise Him is to destroy oneself.

David may be one of few monarchs guilty of just one adulterous affair and one brutal murder. But neither he nor anyone else can defy the law of God with impunity.

31

What are you doing here, Elijah?

(1 Kings 19:9)

Scripture reading: 1 Kings 19:1-21

God had been telling Elijah where to go and what to say. Now the prophet had chosen his own place. Always before, he had accepted divine choices in faith. His own choice was the product of fear.

Elijah had wiped out the prophets of Baal. Enraged, Jezebel issued a death threat against him, and Elijah made a rapid exit from the capital. Here he was, hiding in a cave from the murderous wrath of a pagan woman.

His real problem was battle fatigue and its ensuing depression. God had a remedy—food, rest, work, and a new posting, this time to heaven.

"Hell . . . has no . . . fury like a woman scorned," and heaven has no solace like a God sympathetic, understanding, and appreciative. It was Elijah's lot to be hunted by the one and found by the Other.

Those who risk everything for the Word of God may not escape the wrath of His enemies, but they will survive that wrath, if not in this world, then in one far better.

32

Do you see this vast army?

(1 Kings 20:13)

Scripture reading: 1 Kings 20:1-34

*A*hab was pushed to the limits. Bullied and blackmailed by Ben-Hadad, he finally mustered the courage to say, "No more," and battle lines were drawn.

An unnamed prophet voiced the Lord's question. **"Do you see this vast army?** I will give it into your hand today, and then you will know that I am the Lord" (v. 13).

Indeed, Ahab saw them, and no doubt his eyeballs trembled. To his credit, he acted upon the prophet's word and routed the arrogant invaders. Ben-Hadad was twice-whipped and eagerly proposed and signed a peace treaty.

The Lord is not impressed by boastful threats and large numbers. He determines the future of His people, and He never lowers His flag or yields His sword to an enemy.

Bismarck satirically affirmed that God was on the side of the biggest battalions. Victory belongs to the army that gets there first with the most, according to a Civil War leader. God has delighted in turning such practical wisdom upside down.

33

Have you not murdered a man and seized his property?

(1 Kings 21:19)

Scripture reading: 1 Kings 21:1-29

*A*hab wanted Naboth's vineyard, but Naboth said, "Not for sale." The king, already too rich for good sense, pouted like a spoiled brat. "Cheer up," said cruel Queen Jezebel, "I'll get you the vineyard."

It was easy. False charges were made, swift execution followed the condemnation of the accused, and the property of the deceased was confiscated by the crown. Nothing to it.

Then Elijah faced the king in the stolen vineyard with the word of the Lord: **"Have you not murdered a man and seized his property?** In the place where dogs licked up Naboth's blood, dogs will lick up your blood" (v. 19).

Suddenly all the grapes were sour. No wine from that vineyard would ever cheer the heart of Ahab. Suddenly Jezebel was no business genius. She was a death notice tattooed on Ahab's feverish conscience.

Low-down tricks by high-up folks can never escape the righteous wrath of God. No sinner has immunity from His judgment.

34

Have you noticed how Ahab has humbled himself before me?

(1 Kings 21:29)

Scripture reading: 1 Kings 21:17-29

*G*od's death notice knocked all the strut and boast out of King Ahab. "He lay in sackcloth and went around meekly" (v. 27). The roaring lion became a whipped cur.

God said to Elijah, **"Have you noticed how Ahab has humbled himself before me?** Because he has . . . , I will not bring this disaster in his day, but . . . in the days of his son" (v. 29).

The "disaster" to which God referred was the prophesied destruction of every claimant to the throne from the loins of Ahab.

Judgment deferred is judgment still, and Elijah's grisly prophecy was fulfilled. Ahab was slain in a battle he should never have fought. When the royal chariot was later washed out, the scavenging dogs licked up his blood.

Ahab did not live to see a potential dynasty destroyed, but he made his exit from this world with an enormous load of pain, guilt, and despair upon his withered soul. Even in a seller's market no man ever paid a higher price for a vineyard.

35

Who will entice Ahab into attacking Ramoth Gilead and going to his death there?

(1 Kings 22:20)

Scripture reading: 1 Kings 22:1-40

*T*he question emerged from a vision. Micaiah—brave, truthful, and therefore hated by Ahab—recited the dramatic vision to the unhappy monarch. "I saw the Lord sitting on his throne with all the host of heaven standing around him . . . And the Lord said, **'Who will entice Ahab into attacking Ramoth Gilead and going to his death there?'"** (vv. 19-20). The answer: A lying spirit in the mouth of false prophets would assure the king of victory, thus baiting him to his destruction.

There are always some preachers around who curry the favor of eminent sinners by declaring what those sinners want to hear, not what they need to hear. Such craven preachers call this "being positive."

But always there are some lonely Micaiahs whose ministries wear no price tags. Their consciences are captive to God's Word. They prefer truth to honors.

Lying spirits are applauded, honest prophets are punished, and fools go to their deaths. That has been the stuff of history, and not only in ancient Israel.

36

Is it because there is no God in Israel that you are sending men to consult Baal-Zebub, the god of Ekron?

(2 Kings 1:6)

Scripture reading: 2 Kings 1:1-17

*K*ing Ahaziah was injured by a fall. He sent messengers to consult a pagan idol about his prospects of recovery. By this insult to the true and living God the foolish king blew any chance of getting well.

His emissaries were intercepted by Elijah, who delivered an angry message from the Lord: **"Is it because there is no God in Israel that you are sending men to consult Baal-Zebub, the god of Ekron?** Therefore you will not leave the bed you are lying on. You will certainly die!" (v. 6).

Ahaziah wasted the lives of 2 officers and 100 men to bring Elijah into custody. All he got for his trouble was a ditto of the message. Not only was the blunt prophecy repeated, it was confirmed. Ahaziah "died, according to the word of the Lord that Elijah had spoken" (v. 17).

Is it because the living God has vacated His throne that people today consult gurus, palmists, psychics, astrologers, and other assorted charlatans? The Lord's Word will be fulfilled; the phonies will fail.

37

Who is it you have insulted and blasphemed?

(2 Kings 19:22)

Scripture reading: 2 Kings 19:1-28

*S*ennacherib was contemptuous of all kings, all armies, and all gods. None of them could defeat him. A battle would only mean useless slaughter. Why not surrender and spare the bloodshed?

God sent the boastful monarch a special message: **"Who is it you have insulted and blasphemed?** Against whom have you raised your voice and lifted your eyes in pride? Against the Holy One of Israel!" (v. 22).

God promised to turn Sennacherib back before a single arrow could be shot into Jerusalem. By the next morning 185,000 men were lying dead in the Syrian camp, victims of a killer unidentified to the king but known to us as the angel of the Lord. Arrogant Sennacherib got the message and skedaddled.

Back home, as he worshiped his helpless god Nisroch, he was slain by two of his own sons.

The Holy One insulted, the helpless god honored, and an apostate monarch is sliced up by his own sons. History is ironic. It proclaims and demonstrates that God is not mocked with impunity.

38

Why do you disobey the Lord's commands?

(2 Chron. 24:20)

Scripture reading: 2 Chron. 24:17-25

*J*oash was a weak man. As king he had been guided by a wise and faithful priest, Jehoiada. When his mentor died, he stupidly consented to idolatry to please the politicians—a spineless, greedy breed of men.

Enter Zechariah, son of the deceased loyalist. In the power of the Spirit he thunders the question of God: **"Why do you disobey the Lord's commands?"**

The unspoken answer was money, but Joash would reap no windfall from his dalliance with craven politicians and pagan idols. "You will not prosper. Because you have forsaken the Lord, he has forsaken you" (v. 20).

At the king's order Zechariah was executed in the Temple courtyard. Joash washed away in blood all memory of Jehoiada's kindness. The dying Zechariah exclaimed, "May the Lord see this and call you to account" (v. 22).

Later, wounded in battle, Joash lay helpless on his bed. His officials avenged Zechariah by killing him there.

The gross national product of a nation is never truly served by sin. When religion is falsified to aid the economy, God will call those responsible to account. No people will prosper long who make their gold by forsaking God.

39

*Why do you consult this people's gods,
which could not save their own people
from your hand?*

(2 Chron. 25:15)

Scripture reading: 2 Chron. 25:5-24

*K*ing Amaziah followed a brilliant victory with a stupid decision. He slaughtered the Edomites but then adopted and worshiped their helpless idols.

His idolatry angered the Lord, who dispatched a prophet to say to the king, **"Why do you consult this people's gods, which could not save their own people from your hand?"**

The defiant king silenced the prophet, but not until the messenger of God had declared the king's coming doom.

Today's popular idols can no more save their devotees than could the unseeing, unhearing gods of ancient Edom. The judgment of God upon modern idolatry may be deferred for years, as it was in Amaziah's case, but sooner or later it will come. Prophets can be silenced, but "God is not mocked" (Gal. 6:7, KJV). Seed will come to harvest.

To forsake mankind's only Savior for anyone or anything is to create an idol that can damn but never save its devotees.

40

The Lord said to Satan,
Where have you come from?

(Job 1:7)

Scripture reading: Job 1:1-22

Satan's answer to the above question was, "From roaming through the earth" (v. 7). One who has nothing better to do than chase around looking for someone to slander is on the way to becoming a sub-rate Satan. Here Satan sounds like a reporter for some scandal-mongering newspaper.

Satan's origins are mysterious and unexplained. His access to the council of God troubles some readers of the Bible. It needn't. The record may leave some things unclear, but it makes crystal clear the fact that God is in charge. Satan has access but not authority.

Scripture makes apparent both the power and the weakness of Satan. He can roam, probe, accuse, and harass people ruthlessly, but he answers to God. He cannot escape divine judgment upon his evil actions.

And if he cannot, neither can we, wherever we go, whatever we do, whoever we know. As Martin Luther boldly put it, "He is God's devil." Autonomy is a delusion, a mirage. No devil and no person is autonomous. All must account to God for the gift of life, for its use or misuse.

41

Have you considered my servant Job?

(Job 1:8)

Scripture reading: Job 1:1-22

God gave high marks to Job. "There is no one on earth like him; he is blameless and upright, a man who fears God and shuns evil" (v. 8).

Of course Satan had looked him over, and Satan despised what he saw. Satan spends little time surveying his own subjects. He knows how to hold the cattle he has already roped and branded. He gives them plenty of range, and they do what comes naturally.

But he could only slander Job. "You hedge him about with blessings. Remove the hedge and he will curse You." Satan judges by his own heart. To the impure all motives are suspect, and all actions are devious.

"Every man has his price" is the devil's one text. All else that he says is commentary on it.

God was a character witness for Job. If we were accused by Satan, would we dare call God to the stand as our Character Witness?

42

Where have you come from?

(Job 2:2)

Scripture reading: Job 2:1-10

God asks the same question and gets the same answer: "From roaming through the earth" (v. 2). Nothing constructive occupies the time and energy of the evil one. He simply ranges about being the devil, seeking for prey like a ravenous beast.

He comes before the Lord not out of choice but to report. His freedom is not absolute. He may prowl the length of a long rope, but he is on God's leash. He has to get a permit to test Job.

Why the permit is granted is a mystery that may test our faith, but that it is granted, not seized, should sustain our faith. God sets limits to the activity of Satan and will bring judgment upon that activity.

Like Job, we may not know why evil is loosed like a flood upon us; but also like Job, we can trust God, though He slays us.

Satan is roaming, God is redeeming. We follow one or the Other.

43

Have you considered my servant Job?

(Job 2:3)

Scripture reading: Job 2:1-10

God's repeated question rubs a little salt in Satan's wound. He stripped away the hedge of blessings, and still Job did not sin or charge God with doing wrong. When ruined without reason, the intrepid believer still maintained his integrity.

Satan doesn't concede defeat. Job's misfortunes were heavy, the devil admits, but their weight fell on others. Let Job be afflicted personally, let his flesh and bones scream in anguish, and then he will curse God.

Once more the mystifying permission is granted. Job is afflicted beyond the power of words to describe or console. His shattered wife echoes Satan and urges him to curse God and die. Job names her well—"foolish woman" (v. 10)—but refuses to curse in misery the God whom he blessed in prosperity.

In agony, he will curse the day of his birth, but nothing can induce him to deny God. "Though he slay me, yet will I hope in him" (13:15).

Faith can exceed pain, grief, death, and mystery. Faith can endure what it cannot escape. Job will question, debate, protest, indict, and most of all suffer, but he will continue to believe and hope.

This magnificent sufferer has inspired thousands to dauntless faith in times of inexplicable agony of body and soul.

44

Who is this that darkens my counsel with words without knowledge?

(Job 38:2)

Scripture reading: Job 38—42

God breaks His silence with that question. Then, in rapid-fire sequence the Almighty showers Job with 70 questions that rattle like hailstones on a metal roof.

Most of the questions are closely related, and all of them exalt the wisdom and power of the Creator. They begin with "Who," and the only answer is "God." They begin "Do you" or "Can you" or "Have you" or "Will you"—and the obvious answer is "No."

Job responds with a confession of his ignorance and frailty. In the presence of God he loses all disposition to argue his case, to defend his innocence, to demand explanations, or to protest injustice. Instead, he repents.

None of God's questions explained Job's quandary—why a righteous servant of God endures such awful suffering and sorrow. The divine inference is, "If you are not wise enough or strong enough to operate the natural world, why should you question My operation of the spiritual world?"

As the story ends, Job is hedged again with blessings. As before, however, he serves God because it is right, not because it is rewarding, not because it is reasonable.

In the presence of the Almighty he dropped his questions and demanded no answers. So will we when we meet God.

45

Do I eat the flesh of bulls or drink the blood of goats?

(Ps. 50:13)

Scripture reading: Ps. 50:1-15

God requires sacrifices from His people, not to satisfy a need of His but to meet a need of theirs. He is not served by human needs as though His life must be sustained by their work. He is God, who alone can say, "I have no need" (v. 9).

God is never confused about His identity or insecure about His survival. It is we who, unless we serve God, come vainly to suppose that we *are* gods. It is we who, possessing a few things, imagine that we will never need anything. To us, self-delusion comes easy and self-knowledge comes hard.

Everything belongs to God, and anything becomes ours only as His gift. Ours is the day of trouble, ours is the need to pray. His is the love and power and wisdom that delivers us. And being delivered, we honor Him with our worship, not to remind Him that He is God, but to remind ourselves that we are not.

Amazing grace! The Most High stoops to deliver the least worthy!

46

What right have you to recite my laws or take my covenant on your lips?

(Ps. 50:16)

Scripture reading: Ps. 50:16-23

*T*his is God's question to the wicked who pretend to be righteous. Always there have been persons who play religion in order to work evil. They honor tradition with their mouths but despise it in their hearts. They perform rituals and recite laws and confess covenants because it gives them social status and political influence and commercial advantage.

Such persons mistake the gullibility of people and the silence of God for success. The charade, they suppose, is working. But God pledges to break His silence with accusation, exposure, and judgment. We have seen this divine truth graphically fulfilled in the case of some popular and wealthy televangelists.

To honest worshipers, "the salvation of God" (v. 23); to false worshipers, the judgment of God. Those are the ultimate options. No one is really getting away with pretense.

47

How long will you defend the unjust and show partiality to the wicked?

(Ps. 82:2)

Scripture reading: Ps. 82:1-8

God, presiding over "the great assembly," lashes out at "gods" who are guilty of judging falsely (v. 1). **"How long will you defend the unjust and show partiality to the wicked?"**

We may have trouble identifying the "assembly"—is it some heavenly council or is it some congregation of Jews at worship?

We may have trouble identifying the remiss judges— are they lesser gods or human rulers?

One thing sure, we recognize the evil addressed. Court rulings that favor the rich and powerful, that deny justice to the poor, the weak, the orphaned, the oppressed —this is the sad history of jurisprudence in all countries and in all centuries, including ours.

God will rise up to judge all nations, all rulers, all judges. Those who sold their verdicts to the highest bidders will know the miseries of the lowest hell.

"How long?" Until the curtain falls on human history. Finally, though, the balance will be struck, and justice will be rendered without partiality.

48

Why should you be beaten anymore?
Why do you persist in rebellion?

(Isa. 1:5)

Scripture reading: Isa. 1:2-9

*I*srael was beaten and bruised from head to foot. Her history was a series of worsening rebellions against "the Holy One" (v. 4). The Source of all her blessings had become the Punisher of all her sins. He could not be holy and ignore sin or withhold judgment indefinitely.

Why make a bad situation worse? God is saying. Why take a licking and keep on kicking? Why persist in a suicidal course?

Sin is irrational and pride is obstinate. Rather than submit in a contest of wills, the sinner chooses death, too morally dense to realize that the choice brings ultimate defeat.

Sin isn't cured by punishment, but sin cannot escape punishment. That was Israel's dilemma and God's heartbreak. God is reluctant to punish and delights in mercy, but when mercy is repeatedly despised, punishment becomes mandatory. The Holy One cannot join in evil by ignoring evil.

49

The multitude of your sacrifices— what are they to me?

(Isa. 1:11)

Scripture reading: Isa. 1:2-20

*A*ccused of rebellion against God, Israel points with pride to her religious activity. Sacrifices were offered, prayers were intoned, incense was burned—and all of it as prescribed by the Law.

God saw it. He saw *through* it. **"The multitude of your sacrifices—what are they to me?"**

False worship is no substitute for true repentance. Partial obedience does not excuse radical disobedience. Civil wrong and commercial greed could not be ignored because dishonest power brokers played religion. God had enough of their hypocrisy.

Their worship was attempted bribery. Things are right at church, so don't worry about the wrongs being done at banks and shops and mills and courts.

The Holy One is Lord of all life. He put the issue squarely before the phonies: Life if you repent; death if you persist. How applicable to modern churches!

50

What do you mean by crushing my people and grinding the faces of the poor?

(Isa. 3:15)

Scripture reading: Isa. 3:1-15

*T*he prophet envisions the Lord holding court as the Judge of Israel. Arraigned before Him are "the elders and leaders" (v. 14), who should have set the example for integrity and righteousness. Instead, they had furnished their homes by exploiting the overworked and underpaid poor.

Moral thunder crashes in the challenge of the Almighty. **"What do you mean by crushing my people and grinding the faces of the poor?"** Like grain between millstones, the poor have been squeezed and crushed to provide the luxuries of the rich. God demands an accounting.

God indicts the rich and defends the poor in prophetic literature. A nation's ultimate judgment is determined by its treatment of the poor. What does that forecast for our nation? For our churches? For us?

Throughout history God has sided with the poor, and churches have sided with the rich. The exceptions to that sad rule form the true people of God.

51

What more could have been done for my vineyard than I have done for it?

(Isa. 5:4)

Scripture reading: Isa. 5:1-7

*I*n words of rare beauty, rhythm, and power Isaiah sings of God's vineyard, the favored nation of Israel. God chose the site, cleared the field, planted the vines, guarded their growth, and looked for an abundant crop of choice grapes. Instead, He received a disappointing harvest of bad fruit.

God disclaims all responsibility for Israel's sins. **"What more could have been done for my vineyard than I have done for it?** When I looked for good grapes, why did it yield only bad?"** (v. 4). His goodness and mercy had abounded, only to be despised and misused.

Now the vineyard will become a trampled wasteland. Mercy rejected leaves no alternative but judgment executed.

The ancient message speaks with sobering power to all who call themselves the Lord's people today. Jesus said, "I am the vine; you are the branches" (John 15:5). Disciples who remain in Him bear abundant fruit. Those who do not are lopped off and burned (John 15:1-7).

52

Whom shall I send?
And who will go for us?

(Isa. 6:8)

Scripture reading: Isa. 6:1-13

*I*saiah saw the Lord exalted in holiness. Necessarily, therefore, he saw himself debased by sin. Despairing of life, he cried, "Woe to me!" (v. 5), anticipating the devastating judgment often introduced by the prophetic "woe."

Instead, the divine response was remedial and cleansing. A live coal from the altar purged his unclean lips and prepared the transformed man for prophetic mission. He heard the Lord asking, **"Whom shall I send? And who will go for us?"**

His reaction was immediate and grateful: "Here am I. Send me!" (v. 8). The person who finds mercy wants to share the message of available mercy with others. The person who escapes judgment wants to warn others of impending wrath. Experienced grace creates its own evangelists.

Told frankly that his ministry will have poor success in turning Israel to God, Isaiah still offers himself as God's message-bearer. That any can be reached is reason enough for all trials and suffering involved in the mission.

53

Does the ax raise itself above him who swings it, or the saw boast against him who uses it?

(Isa. 10:15)

Scripture reading: Isa. 10:12-19

*A*ssyria was the tool of God's wrath. He used this militant nation to bring judgment upon others. But proud Assyria rejects the role of divine instrument and credits all victories to its own wisdom and strength.

God upbraids their folly with His question. Does an ax exalt itself above the woodsman? Does a saw rebel against the carpenter? Just that absurd is Assyria's proud denial of its instrumental role. Just that absurd is Assyria's attempt to usurp the prerogatives of God.

The instrument of wrath, because of its arrogance, will become the *object* of wrath. The pomp and glory of Assyria will be consumed like a brier patch on fire. The Holy One will become a flame, a forest fire exploding in strong winds. His destructive anger will leave so few trees standing that a little child could count them.

So, Assyria, who uses whom?

54

How can you say to Pharaoh, "I am one of the wise men, a disciple of the ancient kings?"

(Isa. 19:11)

Scripture reading: Isa. 19:1-25

*T*he Lord is planning to invade Egypt. Before Him idols will tremble and people will collapse. The rulers will be deposed and the workers will be idled as the country sinks into economic chaos.

To the brain trust that advised Pharaoh, God directs a taunting question: **"How can you say to Pharaoh, 'I am one of the wise men, a disciple of the ancient kings'?"** They will not see disaster coming and cannot prevent its results.

God turns history on its ear and makes fools of the experts who search the past, chart the future, and advise the present. The vaunted wisdom of cabinets, councils, and congresses becomes the mouthing of fools, "senseless advice" (v. 11) that means no more than the raving of drunkards who wallow in their vomit.

The Lord will determine the outcome of history and the fate of nations. Horoscopes and predictions are wasted ink from twisted minds. The Word of God endures forever. The wisdom of men papers birdcages.

55

What troubles you now,
that you have all gone up on the roofs,
O town full of commotion,
O city of tumult and revelry?

(Isa. 22:1-2)

Scripture reading: Isa. 22:1-13

Jerusalem was under siege. Its defenders ignored God's call to repentance. Instead, they stockpiled weapons and supplies, strengthened the walls, stored up water, and *partied*, saying, "Let us eat and drink, for tomorrow we die!" (v. 13).

God delivered the city by scaring off the army of Sennacherib. Now those who had resorted to "the atheism of force" celebrate their escape from death, not by worshiping God but by partying again on the rooftops.

Instead of joining the revelry, the prophet turns away to weep. He knows that shameless ingratitude for divine mercy can only result in some future assault upon the city that God will not avert.

Fools who revel in the face of death will die without mercy. Sinners whose courage is a substitute for repentance may die as heroes, but hell holds many heroes. God and not "guts" is the test of truth and honesty and manhood. To deny Him is to destroy oneself, and medals, ribbons, victories, and promotions cannot save the warrior who defies God. Nor can the nation escape judgment whose victories in battle are celebrated by more people in bars than in churches.

56

What are you doing here and who gave you permission to cut out a grave for yourself here, hewing your grave on the height and chiseling your resting place in the rock?

(Isa. 22:16)

Scripture reading: Isa. 22:15-25

S hebna had office, honors, and influence, but he made a fatal mistake. As adviser to the king, he contradicted the word of God voiced through the prophet Isaiah.

Isaiah confronted the powerful politician at the site of a tomb he was preparing for himself. The prestige Shebna enjoyed in life he intends to preserve after death. The Lord interrupts the project with a blunt challenge that identifies the true and final authority in Israel. **"What are you doing here and who gave you permission to cut out a grave for yourself here . . . ?"**

The question is followed by a shocking statement. The Lord will wad him up and toss him into another country, and there he will die. Furthermore, his successor has already been chosen. So fleeting is fame! So certain are the judgments of God upon proud and presumptuous politicians! Or proud and presumptuous anyones.

57

Shall what is formed say to him
who formed it, "He did not make me"? Can
the pot say of the potter,
"He knows nothing"?

(Isa. 29:16)

Scripture reading: Isa. 29:13-21

*T*he question, heavy with irony, is addressed to a group
of Jewish leaders who secretly plotted an alliance
with Egypt in defiance of the word of God delivered by
Isaiah. They had taken great pains to insure the secrecy of
their meetings, discussions, and plans. They thought, God
himself doesn't know what we are doing, much less that
nosy preacher.

The prophet rebukes their folly. You measure God by
your own creaturely limits, he charges. But you are clay; he
is the Potter. Foolish denials notwithstanding, He sees and
hears and knows what you pots are rattling about. More
seriously, He judges the rebellious arrogance of pots who
play at being the Potter.

Their cabal was doomed before it could be finalized.
They could have plotted freely and aloud in the temples of
deaf and dumb Egyptian idols, but the living God of Israel
was aware of all that sprang up in their minds and spilled
out from their lips. He knows everything!

What secrets of yours is He going to bring into judgment?

To whom will you compare me?
Or who is my equal?

(Isa. 40:25)

Scripture reading: Isa. 40:12-31

God has no peer group. He is "the Holy One" and the only One. He is the Creator, and all pagan gods, whether phenomena of nature or products of men, are creatures.

In Babylon, cradle of astrology, stars were regarded as gods who controlled human affairs. The prophet scathingly demotes them. They are an army commanded by the Lord. He calls the roll and each of them responds. Aware of His power, none of them dares go AWOL.

Ancient man called them gods; modern man calls them accidents. Both identify creation in ways that insult the Creator, but He remains incomparably, peerlessly God.

Creation advertises His unlimited power. The verb *bara* occurs over 20 times in Deutero-Isaiah, and God is always its Subject. He only can create. Man merely fabricates. God alone supplies matter and form to what blind and obstinate persons designate gods.

The unwearied Creator can deliver the weakest person who looks to Him for strength. Inspired by this truth, the prophet proclaimed a second Exodus, this time from Babylonian captivity. The incomparable God is the invincible Liberator!

59

Who has stirred up one from the east, calling him in righteousness to his service?

(Isa. 41:2)

Scripture reading: Isa. 41:1-16

*T*he unwearied Creator becomes the inescapable Judge. He summons the nations who vainly suppose that they control the course of history. To these arrogant "movers and shakers" He poses the question: **"Who has stirred up one from the east, calling him in righteousness to his service?"**

God's reference is to Cyrus, whose conquests would include Babylon and whose decree would allow exiles to return to Jerusalem and restore the city and Temple. Ruler of nations, Cyrus was servant of God. God granted his victories and secured his reign.

Who is truly Lord of history? The God who posed the question supplied the answer: "I, the Lord . . . I am he" (v. 4). This Ruler matches power with grace, identifying himself with the helpless as their Savior.

I lived through the days when Hitler mistook himself for God and boasted of a 1,000-year Reich. His armies shook the world and changed the map. But their war machine broke down, and the egomaniac who directed it died with his mistress in a bunker he had labeled impregnable.

God rules.

60

Who is blind but my servant,
and deaf like the messenger I send?

(Isa. 42:19)

Scripture reading: Isa. 42:10-25

*I*srael, as the servant of God, was intended to be a light for the Gentiles, opening their blinded eyes and releasing them from their dark dungeons.

Instead, the servant refused the Word of God, which brings light, and became blind himself. Eventually he was a captive of those he should have freed. What a commentary on the blinding and binding power of sin.

Having punished Israel, however, God now purposes to redeem them. He will lead the blind along unfamiliar and dangerous paths, turning darkness into light before them. He will bring His people home, chastened and forgiven (vv. 14-16).

Greater than sin and the captivity it brings is the grace of God and the freedom it restores.

Jesus came, the true Israel of God. He gave sight to the blind and brought freedom to the imprisoned. The servant of God was none other than God the Servant. Grace is as amazing as it is mighty! Amen.

61

Which of them foretold this and proclaimed to us the former things?

(Isa. 43:9)

Scripture reading: Isa. 43:1-13

Once again the courtroom metaphor is employed. Let pagan nations provide their witnesses and prove that their gods have prophesied and directed the events of history. None of those unseeing, unhearing, and uncaring idols had ever acted to deliver a captive nation.

God's servant, blind and deaf Israel, who had been redeemed and restored by the Lord, could bear witness to Him, the one God, the only Savior.

No foreign god foretold Israel's captivity. No foreign god effected their release. It was the Lord alone who proved that time, space, and history serve His purposes.

Furthermore, no rival god could thwart that purpose. The first challenging question leads to another that clinches the argument: "When I act, who can reverse it?" (v. 13).

Case closed! Court adjourned! Hallelujah!

62

See, I am doing a new thing!
Now it springs up;
do you not perceive it?

(Isa. 43:19)

Scripture reading: Isa. 43:14-28

*N*ever mind the good old days. You don't have to look backward to witness miracles. The God who planned and executed Exodus I is about to stage Exodus II. He who delivered Israel from Egyptian slavery, freeing and shaping a nation to be His people, is going to restore them from Babylonian captivity. On the tough march homeward He will sustain them by fresh miracles—"water in the desert" (v. 20).

You don't have to look back to see God at work. Look around, look ahead, look within! He is liberating, pardoning, and sustaining His people *now.*

Then was great, but it belonged to ancestors. *Now* is greater, for it belongs to us. The past is more than memory; it is inspiration for present faith and future conquest. Don't dwell on the past—exceed it, for God lives and saves *now.*

63

Who then is like me?

(Isa. 44:7)

Scripture reading: Isa. 44:6-8

*T*he purest affirmations of monotheism in the Old Testament are found in Isaiah. This is a choice sample: "I am the first and I am the last; apart from me there is no God. **Who then is like me?** Let him proclaim it" (vv. 6-7).

The Lord flatly denies the existence of any other god. Let those who claim to be gods interpret the past and foretell the future as He does. Let them speak and execute their word as He has. Let them rule and redeem, having founded and sustained a nation, as He has done and is doing.

The Lord's eternity and His people's history attest His unique being and doing. He is the one, true, living God.

To the many names He bears, a new one is added here—"Rock" (v. 8). Strength and durability mark His existence. There is no other Rock. All that is not founded upon Him will be destroyed.

He is the first and the last, the only One who can say, "I am." There were none before Him, there will be none after Him, there have been none during Him. One God—period! He is the Great Unlike.

64

Who shapes a god and casts an idol, which can profit him nothing?

(Isa. 44:10)

Scripture reading: Isa. 44:9-20

With profound scorn idols and idol-makers are labeled "nothing." Man-made gods are ridiculed by the man-making God.

What could be more ridiculous than a carpenter bowing to a block of wood—*leftover* wood at that! Most of it was used to warm his house and cook his meals. From a remaining chunk he fashions a god and kneels before it in worship!

His neighbor, the village blacksmith, prays to a god forged on his own anvil.

In times of trouble, men cry for deliverance to gods who are the product of their own materials, tools, and skills. If the house caught fire, the worshipers would have to save the god!

Such were the gods for whom Israel forsook her Maker, Ruler, and Savior. No wiser, stronger, or truer are the idols of modern civilizations. The products to which people devote their lives today are utterly helpless to save from sin and to give life meaning.

The God who made you offers life. Any substitute gods you make or buy will bring death.

65

Does the clay say to the potter,
"What are you making?" . . .
Woe to him who says to his father,
"What have you begotten?"

(Isa. 45:9-10)

Scripture reading: Isa. 45:1-13

"Woe to him who quarrels with his Maker" (v. 9). This is the only prophetic "woe" directed to Israel by the prophet. The strong denunciation was prompted by an incredible situation: some of the exiles were grousing because God was using Cyrus to effect their freedom and return home.

The grumblers are sharply rebuked for their rebellion and ingratitude. **"Does the clay say to the potter, 'What are you making?'"** The Maker and Redeemer of Israel will not yield His sovereignty to complaining mortals.

God chooses and uses whom He wills. So great is His love that He will not scrap His plans and leave the critics to well-deserved captivity. That love is reflected in Cyrus, also, who accepts and executes the divine mandate at personal cost, not for personal gain.

"Do you . . . give me orders about the work of my hands?" (v. 11). His ancient people tried to and quickly found out who was Boss. Do we ever try to tell God how and by whom to work in our lives? We might as well save our breath to cool our coffee.

66

Who foretold this long ago, who declared it from the distant past? Was it not I, the Lord?

(Isa. 45:21)

Scripture reading: Isa. 45:18-25

*J*udgment upon a number of nations has been decreed. Now God challenges the survivors of those nations to assemble for trial. They must justify their idolatry before Him who declares, "There is no God apart from me" (v. 21).

Once again the test is predictive prophecy. **"Who foretold this long ago, who declared it from the distant past? Was it not I, the Lord?"**

The pagan gods had not foreseen the emergence and conquests of Cyrus, which climaxed in Israel's deliverance from long exile. Only the living God of Israel proclaimed it beforehand and brought it to pass. How majestic is the Creator and Redeemer compared to the helpless gods that crowded the shelves of deluded people!

This God, who had been usurped by impotent idols, now graciously invites His enemies from all nations to turn to Him and be saved! Every knee is destined to bow before Him. The time is coming when His love and power and wisdom will be universally acknowledged. The salvation He offers is as broad as human need! Here is a God worthy of mankind's adoration and homage.

67

*To whom will you compare me
or count me equal? To whom will you
liken me that we may be compared?*

(Isa. 46:5)

Scripture reading: Isa. 46:1-13

*B*el and Nebo, chief gods of Babylon, are treated with withering scorn in the context of this question. Desperate devotees load the gods upon the backs of weary animals in a frantic effort to save the deities from capture. Alas, the plodding beasts are caught, and the helpless gods become prisoners.

In contrast to gods who must be carried is the Lord who carries His people. From birth to old age He sustains them and saves them.

Golden idols are helpless to hear and save those who cry to them in distressing circumstances. They can neither will nor do anything, but God's purposes stand. He does all that He pleases.

Carried gods or the carrying God—religion that burdens or bears—that is always the option of mankind. You must choose between the almighty "I am" or the impotent "it."

68

You have heard these things; look at them all. Will you not admit them?

(Isa. 48:6)

Scripture reading: Isa. 48:1-11

*L*ook at your history, the Lord challenges Israel. I foretold events and brought them to pass. The gods of wood and metal to whom you are attracted, could they do that? Did they do that?

Now, He says, I will tell you of new things, and these also I will bring to pass. Exodus II, soon to take place, will affirm Him as God, the one and only Lord of history, the one and only Redeemer of mankind.

To acknowledge and proclaim this truth becomes Israel's true mission. She must function as God's witness, or the pain of her long exile will be wasted. The context stresses Israel's past failures to hear and bear God's Word. Will she redeem those failures by future obedience? Or will the tragic rebellions of the past be repeated in the future?

A serious challenge is here for the new covenant people of God. We are called to bear witness to Exodus III, to the deliverance of sin's slaves through the atoning sacrifice of Christ. Will we be faithful to the mission?

69

How can I let myself be defamed? I will not yield my glory to another.

(Isa. 48:11)

Scripture reading: Isa. 48:1-15

*I*srael was compelled to endure captivity because of her idolatry and immorality. God was not helpless to prevent the Exile. Indeed, He had decided and arranged that punishment because of her repeated and impenitent violations of His covenant.

The Captivity should have been a furnace of affliction by which Israel would be refined as silver, but it did not have that effect. Instead, she remained loath to hear God's Word and to reciprocate His love.

Why doesn't He simply wipe out the rebellious ingrates? Why doesn't He pour out the full measure of His consuming wrath upon them? One answer suffices—He is merciful for His own name's sake.

He whose name is love delights in pardon. He will not be defamed and robbed of glory by acting out of character. He will be true to himself by graciously forgiving and restoring them. How unlike God were His people! How unlike His people was God! Should I not say "are" instead of were, and "is" instead of was? Do we eagerly hear and obey Him today?

70

Come together, all of you, and listen: Which of the idols has foretold these things?

(Isa. 48:14)

Scripture reading: Isa. 48:12-22

With almost monotonous frequency the Creator of heaven and earth challenges His people to assemble and hear His word. Line up! Listen up!

Again the contrast between the speaking God and the silent idols is emphasized. He acts, while they squat in sightless and senseless passivity. He summons an ally, a servant, to execute His judgment against Babylon. They are unable to defend their turf or to call others to help them.

History is determined when God says, "I have spoken." Neither demons nor humans can invalidate His Word. His right hand founded the earth and stretched out the heavens. No force can withstand that right hand. It upholds those who trust Him and knocks out those who oppose Him.

Meanwhile the dumb idols sit there, unable to watch the fight, much less to throw a punch. So far from being warriors, the false gods aren't even spectators!

71

Where is your mother's certificate of divorce with which I sent her away? Or to which of my creditors did I sell you? Because of your sins you were sold; because of your transgressions your mother was sent away. When I came, why was there no one? When I called, why was there no one to answer? Was my arm too short to ransom you? Do I lack the strength to rescue you?

(Isa. 50:1-2)

Scripture reading: Isa. 50:1-3

God's questions pile up in response to Israel's slanderous charges. Filled with self-pity, the exiles say, God forsook us as a husband divorces his wife. We are like children sold as slaves to pay their father's debts. Our captivity has endured because God is unable to liberate us. Thus, they maligned both His love and power.

Produce the certificate of divorce, God challenges. Name a creditor who could justly claim My children. God forsakes no one; God owes no one.

They knew the truth. Captivity was righteous judgment upon their sins. They forsook God for idols. He came and called through the prophets, but they refused to hear His word and repent of their sins.

God doesn't lack power to rescue them. He is the Creator whom sky and sea obey! Their disobedience is the sole and ample reason for prolonged exile.

We create the need for deliverance by our sins. God creates the possibility of salvation by His grace.

Who are you that you fear mortal men, the sons of men, who are but grass, that you forget the Lord your Maker, who stretched out the heavens and laid the foundations of the earth, that you live in constant terror every day because of the wrath of the oppressor . . . ?

(Isa. 51:12-13)

Scripture reading: Isa. 51:9-16

Second Isaiah begins, "Comfort, comfort my people" (40:1). Here the Lord says, "I, even I, am he who comforts you" (v. 12). These are rare occurrences in the prophetic literature. The prophet's usual mission was to censure the people for their sins and prophesy their punishment. To be given a mandate to comfort must have been a thrill to Isaiah.

The comfort of which he speaks is the deliverance of the captives from their long exile. With God as their Comforter, Israel need not fear the Babylonians. The captors are like grass, mortal and fragile, no match for the eternal Creator of heaven and earth.

"The wrath of the oppressor" should terrify no longer, for the wrath of God, infinitely fiercer, is coming upon those oppressors. Dry the tears. Calm the fears. God is coming to save His people!

The greatest message of comfort ever proclaimed is the gospel of Jesus Christ. It brings hope and inspires faith in those who have been captive to the worst of all oppressors—sin. It brings a freedom that is spiritual and eternal.

73

"And now what do I have here?"
declares the Lord. "For my people
have been taken away for nothing,
and those who rule them mock."

(Isa. 52:5)

Scripture reading: Isa. 52:1-12

*I*srael was not in exile for anything done against her captors. They were in Babylon for something done against
the Lord. His covenants had been violated, His prophets
rejected, His threats of judgment scorned. To punish their
sins, He sent Israel into captivity for 70 years.

The captors are blaspheming God's name. The people
who endure such mockery now, however, will know that
His name is Redeemer and Ruler. He is going to restore
their freedom and return them to Zion.

The phrase "in that day" (v. 6) occurs here for the first
and only time in Second Isaiah. It refers to the day of deliverance and homecoming, to which His people will respond
with shouts and songs of joy.

Babylon had no claim upon Israel. God had merely
used them as His instrument of judgment. Their mockery
will now bring His righteous judgment upon them. He
who punished His own chosen people will not hesitate to
judge others.

74

Why spend money on what is not bread, and your labor on what does not satisfy?

(Isa. 55:2)

Scripture reading: Isa. 55:1-13

*T*his chapter of Isaiah is addressed to exiles who were reluctant to leave Babylon and return to their homeland. They had made themselves "at home" in the foreign place and culture. They had acquired property and were making money. Why leave?

A person's deepest hunger and greatest need, however, is God. A full stomach cannot compensate for an empty soul. Out of God's will, refusing to share His people's mission, they will live and die unsatisfied.

God calls them to repentance, assures them of pardon, and pledges to them a satisfying future that only His enduring and effectual Word can create.

Their response is crucial, and their time for making that response is limited. This is true of all the promises of deliverance in Scripture—they are glorious but they are urgent. Hear! Seek! Live!

Whom are you mocking? At whom do you sneer and stick out your tongue?

(Isa. 57:4)

Scripture reading: Isa. 57:1-13

This passage of Scripture is a blistering indictment of idolaters within Israel. Their sins are heinous—blasphemy, prostitution, infanticide—and all in the name of religion. God hammers their guilty souls with a series of thunderous questions:

"Whom are you mocking? At whom do you sneer and stick out your tongue?"

"In the light of these things, should I relent?" (v. 6).

"Whom have you so dreaded and feared that you have been false to me . . . ? Is it not because I have long been silent that you do not fear me?" (v. 11).

Liars, rebels, and adulterers, He calls them. The enormity of their sins justifies His wrath. His silence will be broken in judgments that will break them. Let them cry out to their idols when destruction comes! Can those man-made gods save? They are so empty that a puff of wind will carry them away—and a hurricane, not a zephyr, is brewing.

God alone affords refuge and security for His people. To desert Him is to doom oneself.

Is this the kind of fast I have chosen, only a day for a man to humble himself? Is it only for bowing one's head like a reed and for lying on sackcloth and ashes? Is that what you call a fast, a day acceptable to the Lord? Is not this the kind of fasting I have chosen: to loose the chains of injustice and untie the cords of the yoke, to set the oppressed free and break every yoke? Is it not to share your food with the hungry and to provide the poor wanderer with shelter—when you see the naked, to clothe him, and not to turn away from your own flesh and blood?

(Isa. 58:5-7)

Scripture reading: Isa. 58:1-14

The Law required fasting on the Day of Atonement. Tradition had added others. For many the fasts were hollow events; people pretended a piety they did not possess.

God scorns these occasional and minimal self-denials, which only briefly interrupted complacent lives. They insult His nature and frustrate His purpose. He calls for religion that adds social action to private worship. Relieve the misery of the oppressed, the homeless, the hungry, and the naked.

Unless self-denial is yoked to social justice, fasting is farcical. God hears and helps His people in times of trouble and expects them to reflect His compassion by serving human needs. Indifference to society's victims reduces religion to mere formality, and God despises that. If you would fast to please Him, be swift to help people.

77

Who are these that fly along like clouds, like doves to their nests?

(Isa. 60:8)

Scripture reading: Isa. 60:1-12

*T*he glory of the Lord will be restored to Zion, shining from there to all points of the compass. Zion will be "an island of light . . . in a sea of darkness," as Page Kelley has expressed it. People from all nations will be attracted to that glory, coming from everywhere to worship Israel's God.

Some people and treasure will be transported to Zion in the ships of Tarshish. With their white sails billowing in friendly breezes, the fleet appears like fleecy clouds and homing doves to the vision of the prophet.

This passage has been read with joy whenever ships have borne Jews to their homeland from dispersal abroad.

It will have complete fulfillment at the close of history, when the New Jerusalem is revealed (Revelation 21—22). The city of God will be a magnet, attracting the redeemed of all nations and all ages to its glory. They will come to worship God in Christ, who ended their days of captivity by His atoning death and risen life.

78

Where is the house you will build for me?

(Isa. 66:1)

Scripture reading: Isa. 66:1-7

*R*ebuilding the Temple was a major project for Jewish exiles returning from Babylonian captivity. God wants them to know that He cannot be *contained* in a temple as pagan gods are. He is the Creator of all that exists, including time and space, and He cannot be limited to them or by them. He transcends all that He fills and dwells in any part of His creation in an accommodated sense only.

To combine His worship with elements of paganism borrowed from their former captors will surely bring future judgments upon the restored people and their Temple.

The Lord's preferred dwelling is not a place but a person—"he who is humble and contrite in spirit, and trembles at my word" (v. 2). The heart of an obedient and trusting person is more magnificent in God's sight than ornate and costly houses of worship.

The destruction of the Temple was a blow to Israel, not to God. The rebuilding of the Temple was a concession to their needs, not to His. He is the Uncontainable!

79

Who has ever heard of such a thing?
Who has ever seen such things?
Can a country be born in a day
or a nation be brought forth in a moment?

(Isa. 66:8)

Scripture reading: Isa. 66:5-11

God purposed to destroy His enemies and establish His people. They are but a remnant, tiny and puny in the eyes of other people, but they will become a nation—a nation "born in a day."

What God brings to birth will be delivered in health. They will be comforted and nourished at overflowing breasts.

The life of God's people, however threatened by furious enemies or perilous circumstances, is assured and secured by His unfailing Word. He pledges peace and comfort and security to His servants.

He can bring a nation to birth in a day. He can guide and guard that nation for a lifetime. His power is adequate for His purpose, and His purpose is congruent with His character.

What is impossible to men is easily and gloriously possible to God.

80

The word of the Lord came to me: "What do you see, Jeremiah?"

(Jer. 1:11)

Scripture reading: Jer. 1:1-12

The prophet's answer to the question was "The branch of an almond tree." The almond tree was nicknamed the "wake-tree," for it was the first of trees to bloom after their winter's sleep.

The Lord said, "I am watching to see that my word is fulfilled" (v. 12). God was awake! He knew what was going on. He addressed current affairs through His prophets and brought His Word to fruition.

Called to receive and transmit the Word of God, Jeremiah needed assurance that his messages would not fail. The high cost of message-bearing tended to create tension and anxiety. Life itself was often at risk for the sake of God's Word.

The prophet was assured that the risk was worthwhile. God would stand to His Word, vindicating the faith, courage, and sacrifice of the one who proclaimed it. That did not mean immunity from torture, prison, or death. It did mean that the Word proclaimed would triumph over all its foes.

Israel's God never slumbered. He kept watch over His Word, and it never returned to Him unfulfilled. In a world of flux and decay the one thing we can always count on is the Word that God has spoken.

81

The word of the Lord came to me again: "What do you see?"

(Jer. 1:13)

Scripture reading: Jer. 1:13-19

*T*his time the prophet saw a boiling pot tilted toward the south. Such pots were common in the yards of the people, as they used to be in rural places in my own youth. The common sight yielded an uncommon message. From the north God would summon kings and armies to bring judgment upon Judah for her sins.

Young Jeremiah had to deliver this unpopular message to rulers and people who would predictably react in anger. He must stand like a fortified city and endure their resentment. And stand he would, for the Lord promised, "I am with you and will rescue you" (v. 19).

God goes with whom He sends. His presence gives courage in the face of opposition and brings joy in the midst of suffering. Jeremiah will experience this many times, as did the other prophets who served the Word of the Lord at the risk—and sometimes the cost—of their lives.

82

*What fault did your fathers find in me,
that they strayed so far from me?
They followed worthless idols and
became worthless themselves.*

(Jer. 2:5)

Scripture reading: Jer. 2:4-12

*T*here was distance between God and Israel. God had not abandoned them; they had strayed from Him. They deserted the true God for false gods. They forsook the God who had saved them from Egypt and planted them in Canaan. Leading them astray were their priests and rulers. The tree died from the top.

What we worship we come to resemble. Like gods, like people. Following the Holy One, they were holy (vv. 2-3). Prostrated before worthless idols, they became worthless.

The rupture between God and His people was not caused by any fault in Him. He was faithful to His covenant. The cause lay in their own corrupt hearts. They swapped gold for mud and went bankrupt.

If God once seemed closer to you than now, who do you suppose has strayed? In whom is the fault located?

83

Has a nation ever changed its gods?

(Jer. 2:11)

Scripture reading: Jer. 2:5-19

*A*n unprecedented sin; an unequaled guilt. Israel exchanged "Glory" for worthless idols. It is enough to shock the heavens, where stars are constant in obedience to their Creator.

Israel's sin was twofold. She committed apostasy— "they have forsaken me"—and idolatry—they "have dug their own cisterns" (v. 13). What consummate folly, to forsake an artesian well of life for cracked cisterns that presaged death.

What is an idol? Anyone or anything to which persons assign the place and value that God should have in their affections and activities is an idol.

Cracked cisterns abound today. People are choking on dust who could be drinking from a spring that never stops flowing. They are ravaged by a thirst for God, which they try to slake at death-producing fountains of money, power, drugs, and sex. Many of them had parents who served God, but they changed their parents' God for idols, and they will never be satisfied until they repent and return to Him.

84

Is Israel a servant, a slave by birth?
Why then has he become plunder?

(Jer. 2:14)

Scripture reading: Jer. 2:13-19

No, Israel was not a slave by birth. "Out of Egypt I called my son," said God (Hos. 11:1). The son has become a slave. Fellowship with a wise and generous Father has given place to cruel exploitation by pagan despots.

How? Why? Another of God's questions supplies the answer: "Have you not brought this on yourselves by forsaking the Lord your God . . . ?" (v. 17).

The spring of life was forsaken for the rivers of Egypt and Assyria. Not trusting God, Israel scrapped the covenant with Him for political treaties with them. The treaty partners became abusive plunderers of the guilty nation.

God, the covenant Partner, became a rejected Deliverer. Sin blinds, degrades, enslaves, and thus invites appropriate retribution. Honest moments require from every sinner under judgment the admission, "We brought it on ourselves."

The oppressed slave can become again the free son. That, however, we cannot bring on ourselves. Salvation is by the grace of God from start to finish.

85

How then did you turn against me into a corrupt, wild vine?

(Jer. 2:21)

Scripture reading: Jer. 2:20-25

*T*he vine metaphor is commonly used for Israel in the Old Testament. God planted a choice vine from good stock in rich soil. He tended it well, yet it became corrupt and wild. How?

A turning occurred. Pagan gods, notoriously capricious, might turn against their devotees. In contrast, Israel's God was faithful and covenant-keeping. He did not turn against His people.

They turned against Him. For no good reason they turned to idols. Sin is, by its very nature, irrational. "They know not what they do," said the Cross-hung Jesus (Luke 23:34, KJV). Sin is moral suicide. Sin acts against the sinner's own best interests.

Jesus said, "I am the vine" (John 15:5). He was the true Israel, the Son of God who would not become a slave to sin, who could not be exploited by His enemies. In Him we see what God's people should have been—loyal to the will of God at any cost.

Israel said, "I will not serve you!" (v. 20). Jesus said, "Your will be done" (Matt. 26:42). The quality of our lives is determined by whether we turn from the Lord of the vineyard or turn to Him.

86

How can you say, "I am not defiled;
I have not run after the Baals"?

(Jer. 2:23)

Scripture reading: Jer. 2:20-25

*S*tained by guilt, Israel could not cleanse herself. Instead, she compounded the guilt by denying the stain. **"I am not defiled; I have not run after the Baals."**

Using an earthy figure, God describes Israel's pursuit of idols as the behavior of a rutting donkey seeking a mate. They plunged into idolatry like an animal in heat. Upbraided by the prophets, they said, "Spare us your sermons. We can't help ourselves. We love these foreign gods, and we will pursue them."

Evil becomes addiction. The addict knows his behavior is self-destructive, but his craving is more powerful than reason or conscience. Whatever the consequences, the "fix" must be obtained.

Israel pursued the lifeless Baals, who could not themselves pursue anyone. Israel was pursued by the living God, who loves even those who turn against Him.

87

*Where then are the gods you made
for yourselves? Let them come
if they can save you when you are in trouble!*

(Jer. 2:28)

Scripture reading: Jer. 2:26-30

*I*srael made gods. They had as many gods as they had towns. When trouble came, not one block of wood or chunk of stone they called "Father" could come to their rescue.

So the people who made gods were forced to appeal to the God who made people. "Come and save us!" they begged (v. 27).

When God taunts them for their folly, saying of their useless idols, **"Let them come,"** the people actually feel cheated. They had simply added these gods to Him; they did not totally substitute other gods for Him. Since they also included Him in their worship, should He not recognize their claim to His intervention?

To their twisted reasoning God responds with another question, posed in legal language: "Why do you bring charges against me? You have all rebelled against me" (v. 29). They have no case. He is not derelict in duty. They are the covenant-breakers, not He.

God will not go on trial at the Judgment; we will. He will not answer to us; we will account to Him. Think about that when you are tempted by idols.

88

Have I been a desert to Israel or a land of great darkness? Why do my people say, "We are free to roam; we will come to you no more"? Does a maiden forget her jewelry, a bride her wedding ornaments? Yet my people have forgotten me, days without number.

(Jer. 2:31-32)

Scripture reading: Jer. 2:31-37

When Israel was faithful to her covenant with God, things were good. There was no slavery, as in Egypt. There were no life-threatening crises, as in the wilderness. They were provisioned, protected, and prospered by the Lord.

Despite all this, they abused their freedom and sought other gods. Like an adulterous wife who abandons a faithful husband, they lusted for heathen deities and customs. Nor was Israel's misconduct a brief fling. She was guilty of a continuous series of affairs—**"days without number."**

"We are free" was a hollow boast. They were prisoners of their lusts and lies, driven to continued evil, though it no longer afforded pleasure. That is every addict's boast and every addict's misery—a freedom that enslaves.

89

Why do you go about so much, changing your ways?

(Jer. 2:36)

Scripture reading: Jer. 2:31-37

*I*n spite" of numberless days of reprehensible conduct, the idolatrous people protest their innocence and refuse to take divine anger seriously. God declares that their judgment is coming precisely because they deny their sin.

"Why do you go about so much, changing your ways?" The *Revised Standard Version* reads, "How lightly you gad about, changing your way!"

The fickle nation refuses to concern itself with the threat of judgment. Have their political fortunes soured with Assyria? No matter—they will seek an alliance with Egypt. Her gods and armies will secure them.

No, says God, you will be disappointed again. He has rejected the allies that Israel trusted, and none of them will come to her aid when disaster strikes. Vain are treaties with men when covenants with God have been dishonored.

God's people cannot trust themselves to political rulers or military forces. Their one Savior is God.

90

If a man divorces his wife and she leaves him and marries another man, should he return to her again? Would not the land be completely defiled? But you have lived as a prostitute with many lovers— would you now return to me?

(Jer. 3:1)

Scripture reading: Jer. 3:1-5

Guilty Israel insists on taking lightly what God takes seriously. Her brazen idolatry has been judged by droughts that threaten famine. Now she wriggles up to God like an adulterous wife confident of persuading an angry husband to relent and turn on the flow of benefits again. She calls him "Father" and "friend" and asks in teasing tones, "Will you always be angry?" (vv. 4-5).

"This is how you talk," God replies. You treat your infidelity like some slight peccadillo, "but you do all the evil you can" (v. 5). What Israel seeks is forgiveness without repentance. She wants favors without obligations. "Take me back," she implores, "with no reproaches, no punishment, and no demands for future fidelity."

In a nutshell, she wants to *use* God, not serve Him. But He will not share His people with idols. He will not give His glory to others. He is a jealous God, and the options are fidelity or divorce. Reconciliation is conditioned upon repentance. He saves from sin, not in sin.

91

During the reign of King Josiah, the Lord said to me, "Have you seen what faithless Israel has done?"

(Jer. 3:6)

Scripture reading: Jer. 3:6-13

*T*he Lord had seen. Nothing good or evil escapes His notice. Had the prophet seen? He could not have missed it. Israel's brazen and repeated infidelities were taking place "on every high hill and under every spreading tree" (v. 6). There was no attempt at secrecy. The real question is, "Have you been sufficiently horrified and saddened by sin to cry out against it?"

Idolatry as spiritual adultery is a common motif in the prophets. Both were capital offenses. Israel had no extenuating circumstances to plead. She had no reason to expect mercy from an offended, betrayed, dishonored God. She deserved only death.

And yet, God sends the prophet to plead, "Return, faithless Israel" (v. 12). He promises to be merciful and forgiving. Indeed, His people's future will be greater than its past. God's presence will be so real and constant that its symbol, the ark of the covenant, will not even come to mind.

What a God! What fathomless love! What measureless mercy! What indescribable tragedy that His offer was refused!

92

Why should I forgive you? . . .
Should I not punish them for this? . . .
Should I not avenge myself
on such a nation as this?

(Jer. 5:7, 9)

Scripture reading: Jer. 5:1-11

Such a nation, indeed! Israel had "favored nation" status with God. He chose them. He freed them from slavery. He "supplied all their needs" (v. 7). He chastened them for wrongdoing and forgave them when they repented. What more could He have done?

Despite all this, they filled the temples of idols, committing spiritual adultery with all the passion of "lusty stallions . . . neighing for another man's wife" (v. 8). From rulers to peasants, the Lord charges, there are no honest dealers, no truth-seekers, in Jerusalem.

In the absence of repentance God cannot forgive sin. Neither can He ignore His people's guilt. They leave Him but one option—to punish sin, and this He will do.

Should He punish? Should He avenge? The obvious answer is yes. How reluctant He was to accept the answer! God takes no pleasure in His people's sufferings, but He cannot sacrifice His own holiness to their infidelity.

93

Should you not fear me?
(Jer. 5:22)

Should I not punish them . . . ?
(Jer. 5:29)

Scripture reading: Jer. 5:14-31

*T*he answer to both questions is an emphatic yes.

Israel should tremble before the power of Him who creates and restrains the sea. They should tremble before the grace of Him who sends them rain and assures their harvest. However, they are unmoved by power and grace alike, refusing to acknowledge the sin that deprives them of good.

God limits the sea, but they put no limits upon their sin (vv. 22-28). They exploit, abuse, and rob one another continually and ruthlessly. They refuse to see the truth or hear God's summons to repentance. Their problem is not ignorance; it is rebellion. They have *preferred* darkness to light.

The Holy One must act in the face of sin. They have not limited sin, but they have limited His options. He must now punish and avenge. To overlook sin would compromise His holiness. He would not be God if He did not judge sin.

So far from fearing Him, they forsook Him.

So far from accepting this, He avenged it.

94

But what will you do in the end?

(Jer. 5:31)

Scripture reading: Jer. 5:30-31

*L*ying prophets and corrupt priests worked hand in hand to encourage and countenance the idolatry and immorality of Israel. Those who should have reproved evil and reformed life conspired instead to profit from the nation's wickedness.

The nation was rotten at the top and the bottom. So far from protesting the failure of their religious leaders, God says, "My people love it this way" (v. 31). Prophet, priest, and people were all in revolt against God.

"But what will you do in the end?" God determines the end of sin, and that means swift, righteous, impartial judgment. The hand that wields the sword of justice cannot be stayed by any coalition or conspiracy of apostates. "The wages of sin is death" (Rom. 6:23) was written long after Jeremiah's time, but it affirms a principle that has always been true. Payday was coming for Israel.

Judgment is a prominent theme in the New Testament also, but a neglected theme in modern preaching. God has not changed, but His prophets have lost courage. Sin is not rebuked, repentance is not demanded. But don't be deceived—payday is coming.

Are they ashamed of their loathsome conduct?
No, they have no shame at all;
they do not even know how to blush.

(Jer. 6:15)

Scripture reading: Jer. 6:1-15

Shame is an index to character. Tell me what shames you, and I will know what sort of person you are. "I am not ashamed of the gospel," said Paul (Rom. 1:16). Israel, laments God, is not ashamed of their sins.

The prophet, "full of the wrath of the Lord" (v. 11), is told to pour it out upon men and women, old and young, great and small, prophets and priests. The entire nation has become too wicked to feel any shame for their idolatry and immorality.

There is no escape from God's wrath when there is no shame for man's wickedness. Those who cannot blush for sin will not pray for mercy and cannot escape judgment. When people choose their gods, they also choose their characters and their destinies.

"Choose for yourselves this day whom you will serve" (Josh. 24:15)—God or the gods. Joshua's ancient challenge is a modern responsibility. Whom do you choose?

96

What do I care about incense from Sheba or sweet calamus from a distant land?

(Jer. 6:20)

Scripture reading: Jer. 6:16-21

*I*srael stubbornly refused to walk in "the ancient paths" of her covenant with God (v. 16). She defiantly closed her ears to the warning trumpets of the prophetic messages. Having deliberately and arrogantly rejected God's Word, she still expected Him to be favorably impressed with rituals that featured expensive and exotic spices.

God could not care less about such religious posturing. No sacrifices can please Him when hearts are not contrite and wills are not obedient. He cannot be manipulated by the rituals of falsehearted and forked-tongued worshipers.

They are bringing incense to Him, but He is bringing disaster to them. They will "perish" (v. 21). His Word must be obeyed, or His wrath must be endured—no middle course exists.

Is it hard for us to understand this? Is it difficult for us to accept the fact that God so earnestly hates and so severely judges sin? If it is, that alone advertises the power of sin to deaden and delude its victims.

Will you steal and murder, commit adultery and perjury, burn incense to Baal and follow other gods you have not known, and then come and stand before me in this house, which bears my Name, and say, "We are safe"—safe to do all these detestable things? Has this house, which bears my Name, become a den of robbers to you?

(Jer. 7:9-11)

Scripture reading: Jer. 7:1-15

No sin was left undone, and yet the perpetrators of gross evil felt secure because the Temple of the Lord stood in Jerusalem and they stood in the Temple. Did it not bear His name? Would He not defend it, therefore, against any foreign invader?

God says, "You are trusting in deceptive words" (v. 8). Unless they repent and reform, He will allow the people to be deported and the city and the Temple to be destroyed. His name is holy. It cannot be used as a cover for sin. It can be invoked for mercy and pardon by sinners who repent, but He never allows it to be a refuge for evildoers seeking to escape righteous judgment.

When the house of God becomes a den of robbers, it will be *their* house, not His, and its ruin will be inevitable. Jesus called the Temple "my Father's house" (John 2:16), but when His authority was rejected, He said, "*Your* house is left to you desolate" (Matt. 23:38, italics added). Think of that, too, when you read, "Your body is a temple of the Holy Spirit" (1 Cor. 6:19).

98

They pour out drink offerings to other gods to provoke me to anger. But am I the one they are provoking? declares the Lord. Are they not rather harming themselves, to their own shame?

(Jer. 7:18-19)

Scripture reading: Jer. 7:16-29

*S*in harms the sinner, not God. He is insulted by it, grieved by it, angered by it, but not harmed. Sin doesn't change God, it changes the sinner, and only and always for the worse.

Sin robs God of nothing, not even His glory, for He is glorified either in forgiving sin or in judging sin. But sin robs the sinner of integrity and liberty. It debases and enslaves. Character and conduct are corrupted by sin.

God remains truly divine, the Holy One, in spite of the world's wickedness. But persons do not remain truly human when they have sinned. Sin creates moral defectives, hideous caricatures of what God intended when He created man in His own image.

To sin is not to harm God but to harm ourselves. To persist in sin is to destroy ourselves. Unless sin is forsaken, God's wrath "will burn and not be quenched" (v. 20). The ashes will be the sinner's, not His.

99

When men fall down, do they not get up?
When a man turns away, does he not return?

(Jer. 8:4)

Scripture reading: Jer. 8:1-7

Content to wallow where they have fallen! Turning from God and refusing to return! Persistence in sin is the hallmark of hardened hearts. Sin hardens, like sunlight on moist clay, until the form created becomes fixed.

Israel had lost all desire to return to God. She raises no questions about her misdeeds. Her conscience has been cauterized. Like horses charging blindly into battle, the people plunge into sin. They have utterly forsaken and forgotten "the requirements of the Lord" (v. 7). Each person is entirely bent on pursuing "his own course" (v. 6).

The sinner's course is downward. Sin's center of gravity is hell. People have completely yielded to the down-dragging force of sin when they fall and refuse to rise.

Jesus told some of those who heard His words, "You refuse to come to me to have life" (John 5:40). Later He said, "Where I go, you cannot come" (8:21). Will not becomes cannot, and judgment becomes inescapable.

100

How can you say, "We are wise,
for we have the law of the Lord,"
when actually the lying pen of the scribes
has handled it falsely? The wise will be put
to shame; they will be dismayed and trapped.
Since they have rejected the word of the Lord,
what kind of wisdom do they have?

(Jer. 8:8-9)

Scripture reading: Jer. 8:4-12

Outraged by the charge of ignorance (v. 7), Israel claims to possess wisdom because they possess the written law of God. Torah is their claim to wisdom.

Wisdom lies in the practice of Torah, however, not in the possession of it. Dust-covered Bibles do not attest the wisdom of sin-laden people.

Israel's scribes, their "wise men," have handled Torah deceitfully. External rituals have been given precedent over moral ethics. The Word of God has been rejected, not as a possession but as a practice, not as a treasured artifact but as a spiritual guide.

Those claiming wisdom will be trapped. Their wisdom is that of an animal baited to its death.

The Word of God studied, believed, and practiced is the true source of moral wisdom. When that Word is scorned or neglected, so-called wisdom is a mask worn to disguise the faces of fools. Their disguises will not allow them to escape their dismay.

101

"See, I will refine and test them, for what else can I do because of the sin of my people? . . . Should I not punish them for this?" declares the Lord. "Should I not avenge myself on such a nation as this?"

(Jer. 9:7, 9)

Scripture reading: Jer. 9:1-11

The nation was so wicked that Jeremiah longed for a place of escape in the desert. He could not bring himself to desert the people, however, and neither could God.

God's judgment upon the nation was inevitable. **"What else can I do . . . ?** His questions, **"Should I not punish . . . ? Should I not avenge . . . ?"** occur several times. This does not argue indecision on God's part. Rather, it reminds the weeping, groaning prophet that Israel had left Him no choice.

The people chase from sin to sin, ignoring His calls to repentance and His threats of judgment (v. 3). They are so treacherous that friends and brothers cannot be trusted (vv. 4-6). What else can God do but bring a refining judgment?

He cannot simply ignore sin—that would be devil-like, not godlike. No, the options are closed and the judgment must fall. Neither God nor His prophet can be unmoved spectators to sin or its punishment. Heartbreak is the cost of loving and caring involvement.

102

What is my beloved doing in my temple
as she works out her evil schemes with many?
Can consecrated meat avert your punishment?

(Jer. 11:15)

Scripture reading: Jer. 11:1-17

*M*y beloved"! The covenant people are such hardened
and persistent sinners that God's judgment upon
them is now inescapable. They use His house as a hatchery
for evil schemes, vainly supposing that their sacrifices will
purchase His favor and placate His wrath. So hopelessly
wicked have they become that God forbids the prophet to
pray for them. He will not listen to their cries for help
when disaster strikes them. And yet He calls them "my
beloved"!

The worst of sins cannot quench the holiest of love.
Man may sink to terrifying depths of iniquity in his defiance of God and concession to lust, but God will still love
him. That boggles the mind; it should capture the heart.
Alas, sin can so corrupt and harden the human heart until
divine love itself becomes an object of scorn.

Holy love acts to forgive sin or to punish it. It must act
or it can be neither holy nor love. Those who despise the
offer of forgiveness can expect only punishment. There is a
cost both to loving and to being loved.

*If you have raced with men on foot
and they have worn you out,
how can you compete with horses?
If you stumble in safe country,
how will you manage in the thickets
by the Jordan?*

(Jer. 12:5)

Scripture reading: Jer. 12:1-6

Jeremiah was pained and puzzled. God was righteous, but life seemed unjust. The wicked prospered, despising God in their hearts while they flattered Him with their mouths. Those who hated and abused the prophet were not punished. Why doesn't God do something to promote equity and justice?

God's response was a question, and the question clearly implied that bad situations would get worse. The prophet will compete with racing horses, not with running men. He will claw through jungles, not walk through open country. Poor Jeremiah! He sought comfort and got challenge. He wanted an easier way and got a tougher route.

The question also implies that small trials and victories prepare for large ones, if a person continues to face inequity and injustice with courageous faith.

God doesn't explain, doesn't apologize. He just calls the prophet to keep trusting, keep serving, keep following, and leave the future to Him.

104

Has not my inheritance become to me like a speckled bird of prey that other birds of prey surround and attack?

(Jer. 12:9)

Scripture reading: Jer. 12:7-13

Jeremiah was hurting. He had faithfully proclaimed God's word to God's people, only to be mocked, rejected, and persecuted.

God was hurting too. His people had become a roaring lion, snarling defiance at the very One who loved and sustained them. Now He will deliver them into the hands of their enemies. The pleasant field will become a wasteland. Armies will swarm over the land as agents of His righteous judgment, leaving countless dead in their wake. And God's heart aches because this must happen.

"Birds of a feather flock together" runs an ancient adage. Birds *not* of a feather fight each other. Israel will become a strange bird, savagely pecked and clawed to death by other birds. She will be the hapless prey of pagan nations.

Israel was God's **"inheritance,"** and He cannot view with pleasure her destruction. Sometimes it deeply hurts to be God!

105

Who will have pity on you, O Jerusalem?
Who will mourn for you?
Who will stop to ask how you are?

(Jer. 15:5)

Scripture reading: Jer. 15:1-9

God had been discarded like a useless piece of broken pottery. His people walked away from Him. Defiance toward Him and distance from Him increased together.

Now they must be punished. They will be winnowed in judgment, blown from their land by His fury against evil. Countless women will become widows as invading armies slay their husbands. Compassion is no longer an option for God.

They despised His caring love, but who will have pity on them now?

The answer is, He will. He will severely punish them, but He will not utterly forsake them. Someday He will restore them to their homeland. Someday Jerusalem will be rebuilt. When no one else cares, the very One whom they rejected will continue to bear them in His heart. The love of God is invincible, surviving all changes, enduring all sins. The love they despised is all that assures them a future. Change "them" to "us," and the message is equally true.

106

Can a man break iron— iron from the north—or bronze?

(Jer. 15:12)

Scripture reading: Jer. 15:11-20

*S*ome versions of Scripture treat this as Jeremiah's question to God. The meaning then would be, "Can I endure the suffering imposed unfairly upon me because I have faithfully proclaimed Your word to a defiant and resentful people?"

The *New International Version* renders this difficult verse as God's question to Jeremiah. The meaning then is, "Who can withstand or endure the judgment I am bringing upon word-rejecting Israel, using as my instrument of punishment a powerful and cruel army from a country to the north?"

In either case, the prophet suffers for proclaiming the word, the people suffer for disclaiming the word. Better the prophet's pain than the people's, for God will reward him but punish them.

To preach an unpopular message from God or to join a popular revolt against God are both costly. In this world, the question is not, How can I escape suffering? but, What shall I suffer for? The next world hinges upon our answer.

107

O house of Israel, can I not do with you as this potter does?

(Jer. 18:6)

Scripture reading: Jer. 18:1-10

*T*he prophet watched the potter and saw God at work. When flawed clay spoiled the potter's vessel, he reshaped it into another pot.

The sin of man seems to argue against the sovereignty of God, but He is the Potter, and we are the clay. He shapes us; we do not shape Him.

The judgment of God upon sin seems to argue the doom of man, but the Potter breaks the clay, removes the flaw, and then refashions it as He wills.

Israel's stubborn rejection of mercy will make judgment—the Babylonian Captivity—inevitable. However, a wise and loving God will restore His people, creating anew a vessel for His purpose.

What was true of Israel as a people is true of today's individuals also. God can remake what sin has spoiled. His love is invincible and creative. Sovereign grace, not evil, has the last word.

Inquire among the nations: Who has ever heard anything like this? A most horrible thing has been done by Virgin Israel. Does the snow of Lebanon ever vanish from its rocky slopes? Do its cool waters from distant sources ever cease to flow? Yet my people have forgotten me; they burn incense to worthless idols.

(Jer. 18:13-15)

Scripture reading: Jer. 18:11-17

*P*agan gods were worthless, but their devotees remained loyal to them. Israel's God was the true and living God, a constant Benefactor to His people, yet they had forsaken Him for idols.

The idolatry of Israel was unnatural. It had no precedent in history, no parallel in nature. The snow-capped peaks of Lebanon were a dependable source of cool, refreshing streams that watered the valleys below. They formed an accusing contrast to the wickedness of capricious Israel.

So unnatural, so unprecedented is Israel's idolatry that comparatives will not serve the prophet; he must choose a superlative—**"a *most* horrible thing"** (emphasis added).

Such unparalleled sin calls for the severest judgment. God will turn His back upon them in their day of disaster. In Scripture, ultimate blessing occurs when God turns His face toward His people. Ultimate disaster occurs when He turns His back on them.

109

Does it make you a king to have more and more cedar?

(Jer. 22:15)

Scripture reading: Jer. 22:13-19

*T*he courageous prophet faces the corrupt king. Jehoiakim, exploiting forced labor, is building an elaborate palace. Jeremiah dares to pronounce a prophetic "woe" against him for his vanity and cruelty.

True royalty consists, not of ostentatious display, but of loyalty to God and concern for the people, as Jehoiakim should have learned from his father's worthy example. "Is that not what it means to know me?" asks God (v. 16).

Any man's first business is to know God, and knowing God means living for others, not for oneself. Looking out for number one may seem financially clever, but it is morally stupid.

For his wickedness, Jehoiakim will die unloved and unmourned. There will be no state funeral for him who so loved pomp and pageantry! Without ceremony, he will be dumped on the garbage heap like a dead donkey. A worse fate is hard to imagine for any ancient Jew, much less an ancient monarch.

110

*Which of them has stood in the council
of the Lord to see or to hear his word?
Who has listened and heard his word?*

(Jer. 23:18)

Scripture reading: Jer. 23:16-24

*I*srael was on the brink of disaster. Nevertheless, lying prophets, eager for acceptance, were filling the impenitent people with false hopes. They dared to preface their lies with the prophetic formula, "The Lord says . . ." Fully aware of the idolatrous nation's guilt, they declared, "You will have peace."

God emphatically denies being the source of their messages. They have not been in His council to hear His word. He sends a true prophet to proclaim a contradictory message. His anger will burst upon the wicked like a storm. The whirlwind of judgment will not abate until His purposes have been fully accomplished.

The false prophet is easy to detect. He preaches what people want to, not what they need to hear. He listens to popular notions, not to divine counsels. His ear is to the ground, not to the heavens. He doesn't thirst for God; he itches for money, money, money. You can hear some of them on television anyday.

"Am I only a God nearby," declares the Lord, "and not a God far away? Can anyone hide in secret places so that I cannot see him?" declares the Lord. "Do not I fill heaven and earth?" declares the Lord.

(Jer. 23:23-24)

Scripture reading: Jer. 23:16-29

*T*he lying prophets who inspired false hopes were treating the Lord like some local pagan idol—too limited in knowledge to know what was happening abroad, too limited in power to pose a threat to His own area. He could be safely ignored or belied.

The Lord thunders against them, proclaiming His omnipresence and omniscience. He sees all, knows all, and governs all. From Him none can hide, none can escape.

God is everywhere, filling heaven and earth. He is not a presence merely, but an Actor, the living God who speaks and acts as Lord of history.

Nothing good or evil escapes His notice or lacks His response. He is there and He is in charge, a truth that we may accept to our comfort or refuse to our destruction.

112

"Is not my word like fire," declares the Lord, "and like a hammer that breaks a rock in pieces?"

(Jer. 23:29)

Scripture reading: Jer. 23:25-32

Lying prophets stole sermons from one another—petty larceny indeed!—and peddled their dreams as revelations from God. As a consequence, God was defamed and the people were deluded.

"How long will this continue?" God asks. The answer is until His word of judgment is fulfilled. That will silence and destroy the lying rascals.

And that word will be fulfilled! It is like wheat compared to the wind-blown chaff of false prophecy.

His Word is irresistible in power, a fire that consumes everything that opposes it, a hammer that smashes the hardest lies that counterfeit it.

Woe, then, to the windbag to whom the God of that word says, "I am against you." Human opinion and eloquence may lull God-forsaking people to sleep in their sins, but they will awaken to the sound of flames crackling and hammers pounding.

113

What do you see, Jeremiah?

(Jer. 24:3)

Scripture reading: Jer. 24:1-10

*T*he prophet saw two baskets, each filled with figs. One contained good, edible figs. The other contained bad, inedible figs.

God explained the vision. The good figs represented exiles who would be preserved and protected, though in a foreign culture. God purposed to restore them at length to their homeland and to himself. With this remnant of Israel the covenant would be renewed.

The poor figs represented Zedekiah and the survivors under his rule. Some would remain in the land, some would migrate to Egypt. Unfaithful to God, they were destined for destruction. Israel's future would not include them.

Through common things God proclaimed uncommon truth. Through material things He communicated spiritual truths. Creation is "sacramental"—capable of functioning as a means of grace. At God's behest, any part of nature may become a channel of revelation.

114

*See, I am beginning to bring disaster
on the city that bears my Name,
and will you indeed go unpunished?*

(Jer. 25:29)

Scripture reading: Jer. 25:15-31

God was going to punish Israel severely for her sins. Surrounding nations, who had sinned with and against Israel, would be judged also, for God rules over all the earth.

Jeremiah introduces a concept that will be repeated often in Scripture—the cup of God's wrath. He is told to bear this bitter wine to other nations, especially to their rulers. All of them must drink it.

The nations may decline, but God says, "You must drink it!" (v. 28). If He would bring disaster upon His own people, can others expect to be spared? "You will not go unpunished, for I am calling down a sword upon all who live on the earth, declares the Lord Almighty" (v. 29).

The God of the Bible is Lord of all time, all space, all people, all history. There is one God, and He makes the same response to all impenitent sinners—His cup of wrath. The water of life or the wine of wrath are the ultimate human destinies. Each nation, each person, will drink one or the other.

115

*Serve the king of Babylon, and you will live.
Why should this city become a ruin?*

(Jer. 27:17)

Scripture reading: Jer. 27:1-22

*T*he lying prophets sounded like superpatriots. They urged resistance to Babylon and promised victory to those who rebelled.

Jeremiah sounded like a defeatist at best, a traitor at worst. Obedient to the Lord, he was compelled to urge submission to a foreign ruler.

The Lord was giving kingdoms to Nebuchadnezzar. To rebel against him, therefore, was to oppose God's purpose. This was a hard message to transmit; it was bound to bring persecution to the messenger.

History vindicated the prophet—but a later generation would be reading that history. Events do not flow swiftly enough to make the true prophet popular in his own time and place. The prophets are killed by their contemporaries; their tombs become shrines only to later generations.

God's Word is costly for Him to speak, costly for people to accept and proclaim. The ultimate price of loyalty to God's purpose was Calvary. The ultimate vindication awaits the Second Coming.

116

Ask and see: Can a man bear children?
Then why do I see every strong man
with his hands on his stomach
like a woman in labor,
every face turned deathly pale?
How awful that day will be!

(Jer. 30:6-7)

Scripture reading: Jer. 30:1-11

A terrible day of judgment is coming—the fall of Jerusalem and the captivity of Israel. Strong men will react to it physically like women gripped by labor pains!

Yet Jacob "will be saved out of it" (v. 7). He will not be spared from it—the devastation will occur—but he will be saved out of it. One day the exiles will return, and Jerusalem will be restored.

God's last word is grace. Divine love is neither capricious nor vincible. God will keep His word to punish, but He will also keep His promise to restore. History, viewed from the human perspective, seems to be in constant and often unpredictable flux, but the Word of God will be fulfilled. That unfailing Word, and not the whims of human leaders, is the real determinant of history.

117

Is not Ephraim my dear son, the child in whom I delight?

(Jer. 31:20)

Scripture reading: Jer. 31:15-20

*C*hapter 31 of Jeremiah is radiant with hope and promise of restoration from exile.

The reason for exile was found in the people. They had forsaken the Lord for idols, with all the consequent immorality that slandered His name and aroused His wrath.

The reason for deliverance, however, is not found in them but in God. "I have loved you with an everlasting love" (v. 3). "He who scattered Israel will gather them" (v. 10). He will make a new covenant with them (v. 31).

They will repent and He will forgive. This does not mean that repentance merits forgiveness. Forgiveness is freely granted to undeserving sinners because God bears toward wayward children a good father's heart of love. Therefore, He has compassion upon His **"dear son,"** who has acted like anything but a son.

Back then, or here and now, the sinner's only hope is created, not by the sincerity and intensity of his penitence, but by the steadfast love of God.

118

I am the Lord, the God of all mankind. Is anything too hard for me?

(Jer. 32:27)

Scripture reading: Jer. 32:6-41

*J*eremiah was commanded by the Lord to do a strange and surprising thing. He was to buy property in a city under siege, a city doomed to become ruins.

He made the purchase, sealed the deed, and had it carefully deposited for preservation. He acted upon God's promise of Israel's future restoration.

When Jeremiah committed the apparently unreasonable transaction to God in prayer, the Lord responded with a consoling question: **"Is anything too hard for me?"** The prophet had already affirmed this truth in his prayer: "Nothing is too hard for you" (v. 17).

God is able to scatter and to gather, to slay and to make alive, to punish and to forgive, to bankrupt and to prosper. And to accomplish His purposes, He is able to control persons, nations, events, and results across decades of time and generations of people.

Nothing is too hard for God!

119

Will you not learn a lesson and obey my words?

(Jer. 35:13)

Scripture reading: Jer. 35:1-19

*J*eremiah was given a strange assignment. At God's instruction, he offered wine to the men of the Recabite family. They declined it out of respect for, and in obedience to, Jonadab—a forefather who had pledged the clan to permanent abstinence.

The lesson was applied to the men of Judah. The Recabites were loyally obedient to an earthly father, but Judah was defiantly disobedient to the Heavenly Father.

As a consequence of their rebellion, God was going to bring upon Jerusalem every disaster He had forewarned. The Recabites, however, would be preserved.

Failing to learn a lesson in obedience, the men of Judah had to learn a lesson in judgment. Either God's word of command will direct our lives, or His word of judgment will punish us. One way or another, His word is the last word.

Trying to get the last word is a human game. God doesn't play the game—He *has* the last word.

120

Why bring such great disaster
on yourselves ... ?
Why provoke me to anger ... ?
Have you forgotten the wickedness
committed by your fathers ... ?

(Jer. 44:7-9)

Scripture reading: Jer. 44:1-30

A remnant of Judah, in disobedience to God's command, sought refuge in Egypt. There they practiced
idolatry in defiance of the prophet's pleas and threats.

When God forbade their going to Egypt, their response
was obstinate and rebellious. "We will not listen . . . ! We
will certainly do everything we said we would" (vv. 16-17).
Opposing their words to the words of the Lord, off they
marched to the forbidden country.

An angry God announced their doom: "The Jews in
Egypt will perish by sword and famine until they are all
destroyed. Then [they] will know whose word will stand—
mine or theirs" (vv. 27-28).

Sin's bravado is hot air. God's Word will stand, though
heaven and earth fall, as Jesus taught. Contradicting that
invincible Word is surely the ultimate human folly. You can
deny, defy, deride, and distort God's Word, but you cannot
defeat it.

121

Should you then seek great things for yourself?

(Jer. 45:5)

Scripture reading: Jer. 45:1-5

*B*aruch, loyal friend and secretary to Jeremiah, was discouraged. The messages of the prophet, which Baruch had helped to circulate at personal cost, seemed to doom his own dreams and prospects of success.

To the depressed man God sent a personal message: "I will overthrow what I have built and uproot what I have planted, throughout the land. **Should you then seek great things for yourself?** Seek them not. For I will bring disaster on all people, declares the Lord, but wherever you go I will let you escape with your life" (vv. 4-5).

God's "losses" were greater than Baruch's, and His pain went deeper. This was no time for personal ambition or self-pity. Baruch could count on something more valuable than material wealth or social status—the presence and protection of God during the coming disasters. He would have the best of friends in the worst of times. Who would not settle for that? And beyond that was the glorious future that God has prepared for His faithful servants!

122

Who is this that rises like the Nile,
like rivers of surging waters?

(Jer. 46:7)

Scripture reading: Jer. 46:2-12

*T*he overflowing Nile controlled the economy and politics of Egypt. Its annual surge becomes a metaphor for Egypt's armed forces, who are ambitious for world conquest.

They will not succeed. God has decreed their defeat by the Babylonians. Euphrates will absorb the Nile! The Lord will offer Egypt there as a sacrifice. The ancient battle of Charchemish was no accident of history—it was the Lord's "day of vengeance . . . on his foes" (v. 10).

A nation or a person can become a friend or foe of God. His friends will be eternally rewarded. His foes are doomed to destruction.

Men often relate themselves to God, to His people, and to His house because they seek human favors or fear human enemies. There is no true friendship with God in such situations, only a futile attempt to exploit Him. He is willing to be a friend to all but the tool of none.

123

Why will your warriors be laid low?

(Jer. 46:15)

Scripture reading: Jer. 46:13-26

*N*ebuchadnezzar was leading his army south to attack Egypt. God, who had decided to offer Egypt as a sacrifice to Babylon, sent the Egyptians a message through Jeremiah: **"Why will your warriors be laid low? They cannot stand, for the Lord will push them down"** (v. 15).

Total defeat is prophesied. Egypt's troops, angry and disgusted when it happens, will brand their Pharaoh a hot-air merchant, a braggart who missed his opportunity for conquest. The people are told to pack their belongings for exile. Proud Memphis, home of Apis, the bull-god, will become uninhabited ruins—unless you count such creatures as beetles, snakes, and owls!

Egypt's defiance of God, Egypt's cruelty to His people, could not go unpunished. The Lord of history chose the time, place, and instrument of punishment. He is in charge.

You won't read anything like that in the newspapers, but that is what's really going on in world affairs today.

O remnant on the plain,
how long will you cut yourselves?

(Jer. 47:5)

Scripture reading: Jer. 47:1-7

*I*t is Philistia's turn to be judged, and Egypt is "the sword of the Lord" (v. 6). The situation will become so desperate that fathers will be helpless to save their children. Deep despair will overwhelm the Philistines. "Gaza will shave her head in mourning. Ashkelon will be silenced" (v. 5).

"O remnant on the plain," God asks, **"how long will you cut yourselves?"** To impress and implore their gods, the soldiers signaled their distress by shaving their heads and cutting their flesh. This is reminiscent of the behavior of the prophets of Baal on Mount Carmel (1 Kings 18:28).

The soldiers respond to God's question with their own tortured cry: "Ah, sword of the Lord, . . . how long till you rest?" (v. 6). The answer is blunt and simple—not until the Lord's purpose to avenge His name upon Philistia is fully accomplished.

Once again central truth in Jeremiah is affirmed as event: God is the Lord of history.

125

How can you say, "We are warriors, men valiant in battle"?

(Jer. 48:14)

Scripture reading: Jer. 48:1-17

Moab was complacent, settled "like wine left on its dregs" (v. 11). The fate suffered by other nations had not perturbed her. She trusted in Chemosh (her number one god) and in her elite troops to preserve her peace.

God had a jolt for her. He was sending invaders to tilt the jars and decant the wine. Chemosh would be exposed as helpless, and the troops would be slaughtered.

"How can you say, 'We are warriors, men valiant in battle'?" How idle to boast of your strength when God has decreed your downfall! History is filled with such empty boasts, but arrogant sovereigns and confident armies have often fallen, and national boundaries have proved elastic.

God can dehorn the mightiest (v. 25), and He can choose the unlikeliest to achieve His purpose. He turns vaunted wisdom to folly, boasted strength to frailty. As a faithful French preacher declared at the funeral of his king, "Only God is great."

126

Was not Israel the object of your ridicule?
Was she caught among thieves,
that you shake your head in scorn
whenever you speak of her?

(Jer. 48:27)

Scripture reading: Jer. 48:20-30

Why the collapse of Moab? Why the destruction of her rulers, armies, and citizens? God supplies the reason: "She . . . defied the Lord" (v. 26).

When Israel went into exile, the Moabites scorned their misery and cheered their tormentors. In ridiculing Israel, they were defying God, for He had chosen the time and place and means by which His people would be judged for their sins. Now the wheel has turned full circle, and Moab will learn by experience what Israel has suffered. Defiance of God is an exercise in self-destruction.

God takes no sadistic pleasure in the suffering He inflicts. Rather, He weeps for Moab (v. 32), laments her desolation (v. 36), and offers her a future (v. 47).

God's *holy* love demands that sin be punished. His holy *love* demands that the penitent remnant be forgiven and restored.

127

Has Israel no sons? Has she no heirs? Then why has Molech taken possession of Gad? Why do his people live in its towns?

(Jer. 49:1)

Scripture reading: Jer. 49:1-6

*I*n 733 B.C. Tiglath-pileser III, king of Assyria, captured parts of the kingdom of Israel and deported the inhabitants. Neighboring Ammonites exploited the situation, taking possession of the vacated areas. There they worshiped their hideous god Molech, who could only be placated by human sacrifices.

Israel had sons. There were legitimate heirs to the empty towns. The Ammonites were usurpers, robbers. Now God is poised for judgment upon the squatters' wrongs. The tables will be turned, and the Ammonites will be beaten, pillaged, and exiled.

To proud Ammon the Lord says, "Why do you boast of your valleys . . . so fruitful?" (v. 4). The riches of Ammon cannot purchase immunity from His judgment. No nation that God has marked for judgment has adequate defenses against His purpose.

Don't miss the "afterward" in verse 6. God's last word will be spoken in mercy, not in wrath.

128

Is there no longer wisdom in Teman?
Has counsel perished from the prudent?
Has their wisdom decayed?

(Jer. 49:7)

Scripture reading: Jer. 49:7-11

*T*he Edomites had a reputation for wisdom. When God moves against Edom in judgment, however, neither her wisdom nor her warriors will be able to save her.

The disaster will be complete. "If grape pickers came to you, would they not leave a few grapes? If thieves came during the night, would they not steal only as much as they wanted? But I will strip Esau bare" (vv. 9-10).

Other nations, less deserving of punishment, had been compelled to drink God's cup of wrath. "Why should you go unpunished?" (v. 12). The answer is obvious, and God asserts that Edom will become a ruin.

Like a roaring lion He will "chase Edom from its land" (v. 19). This is one lion who cannot be driven from its victim. "Who is like me and who can challenge me? And what shepherd can stand against me?" (v. 19).

The Lord will swoop down upon Edom like an eagle, and the nation will be helpless. Before Him the sages will be senile and the warriors will be weak. The mighty are no match for the Almighty.

Son of man,
do you see what they are doing . . . ?

(Ezek. 8:6)

Scripture reading: Ezek. 8:1-18

*E*zekiel was taken "in visions of God" to Jerusalem (v. 3). Four times the Lord asks, **"Do you see what they are doing?"** Each time the prophet sees the "detestable" idolatry being practiced by the Jews, practiced even within the Temple.

To apostate Israel this paganism is "a trivial matter" (v. 17), but it provokes the Holy One to anger. He will not spare them from judgment; they have gone too far. "Although they shout in my ears," God says, "I will not listen to them" (v. 18). Their false gods could not hear; the true God would not hear. They were goners.

From the outset of his ministry Ezekiel learned that God takes sin seriously and judges it severely. The Word of the Lord the prophet ate (3:1-10) was the diet his nation rejected. Their sins, committed not in ignorance of God's Word but in defiance of it, are the cause of all the disasters predicted for them. "God is not mocked" (Gal. 6:7, KJV). No person, no nation, sins with impunity.

130

Son of man, did not that rebellious house of Israel ask you, "What are you doing?"

(Ezek. 12:9)

Scripture reading: Ezek. 12:1-16

*E*zekiel was frequently called to act out a message. In this way he was made a "sign" to Israel.

One day, in public view, he packed his things for exile. That evening, as neighbors watched, he dug through a wall of his house, shouldered his baggage, and walked away.

In the morning God asked, **"Son of man, did not that rebellious house of Israel ask you, 'What are you doing?'"** He was to answer their curiosity with a blunt announcement of coming judgment. "As I have done, so it will be done to them. They will go into exile as captives" (v. 11).

The prophet must live messages as well as preach them. His whole being and his total lifestyle are captive to the Word of the Lord. That Word will sometimes be painful for him to bear, painful for others to hear, for it is the Word of the Lord who will not wink at sin, who will not spare the sword. "The way of transgressors is hard" (Prov. 13:15, KJV); that makes the way of prophets hard also.

131

Son of man, what is this proverb
you have in the land of Israel:
"The days go by and every vision
comes to nothing"?

(Ezek. 12:22)

Scripture reading: Ezek. 12:21-28

*B*ecause threats of judgment were not immediately carried out, the people regarded them as invalid. Ezekiel must warn the scoffers that the days of outpoured wrath are drawing near. Soon God will fulfill all that He has spoken.

Instead of improving the interval by repenting of their sins and imploring God's forgiveness, the hardened people adopted the suicidal attitude that judgment delayed was judgment canceled.

The same folly is described and condemned in the New Testament with respect to the coming again of Jesus Christ to judge the world in righteousness (2 Pet. 3:3-10). But, warns the apostle, "The day of the Lord will come" (v. 10). The "delay" was intended as an opportunity for repentance. It has been treated instead as an occasion for mockery.

The Lord keeps His own calendar, with a day marked for the judgment. It will come, ready or not!

132

*When the wall collapses,
will people not ask you,
"Where is the whitewash
you covered it with?"*

(Ezek. 13:12)

Scripture reading: Ezek. 13:1-16

*F*alse prophets opposed Ezekiel and deceived the people. They preached "peace" in the face of a gathering storm of judgment. God calls them "jackals among ruins" (v. 4). Like hungry beasts they batten upon the people who will fall victim to the very disasters these false prophets denied.

Their pleasant promises are a flimsy wall whose weakness has been disguised by a coat of whitewash. God confronts them in Ezekiel to warn that He is bringing a storm of judgment upon their lies. Furious wind, hail, and rain will level the wall. When it collapses, disillusioned people will ask in anger, **"Where is the whitewash you covered it with?"**

Every denial of God's Word is whitewash smeared on a tissue of lies. His Word will stand when every wall of delusion and deception crumples under judgment. The storms will come, and the only refuge is God's Word believed and obeyed. We cannot prevent the storm; we can accept the refuge.

133

Will you ensnare the lives of my people but preserve your own?

(Ezek. 13:18)

Scripture reading: Ezek. 13:17-23

*T*he question above is addressed to certain women who practiced magic in Israel. They are identified as religious conartists, trappers of souls, whose motive is personal profit. They preyed upon ignorant and fearful persons in order to control the lives and the purses of these gullible victims.

To God this was an insult, a profaning of His name, which called for vengeance. These "religious leeches gorging themselves upon the fears of simple folk"—to borrow a phrase from John Bunn—will be stripped of their charms and veils, thus losing their power to impress and delude the naive. "I will set free the people that you ensnare like birds," says God (v. 20).

Particular details of that ancient situation may be obscure, but the same sort of thing persists today. Those who write horoscopes, read palms, and sell lucky charms and lucky numbers are the same breed of cat.

This passage also brings a word of judgment against television preachers who become multimillionaires by preying upon the fear, or greed, or uninformed desire to do good of dupes who finance their religious racketeering. God's "woe" condemns all such charlatans.

134

Should I let them inquire of me at all?

(Ezek. 14:3)

Scripture reading: Ezek. 14:1-11

Some of Israel's elders visited Ezekiel, hoping to receive a message from the Lord.

God accused them of having set up idols in their hearts and stumbling blocks before their faces. Inwardly and outwardly they were idolaters.

He gave the prophet a blunt message for them—"Repent." Unless they repent, which includes the renunciation of idols, God will destroy both those who inquire and any prophet who claims to give them a message from Him.

God's stated purpose in executing these judgments is "to recapture the hearts of [his] people" (v. 5). That He should even want them, after they have forsaken Him for idols, is a powerful testimony to enduring divine love.

God knows our hearts. He is aware of the motives behind every action. To come to Him insincerely is to invite our own destruction. He will not share our hearts with other gods. He will act, in judgment and in grace, to capture our hearts for himself. That is what He did at Calvary.

Son of man, how is the wood of a vine better than that of a branch on any of the trees in the forest? Is wood ever taken from it to make anything useful? Do they make pegs from it to hang things on? And after it is thrown on the fire as fuel and the fire burns both ends and chars the middle, is it then useful for anything? If it was not useful for anything when it was whole, how much less can it be made into something useful when the fire has burned it and it is charred?

(Ezek. 15:2-5)

Scripture reading: Ezek. 15:1-8

Wood from wild or unproductive vines was good only as firewood—and not much good for that!

Israel, God's vine, had become useless through its idolatry and immorality. It will be consigned to the fire—to the judgment of captivity. Those who survive the fall of Jerusalem, still impenitent and useless, will perish in a further judgment.

Only when His people repent can the Lord make anything useful from them.

Has God's labor for His vine been utterly wasted? No. "When I set my face against them, you will know that I am the Lord." Lordship expressed as mercy had been despised. When experienced as judgment, it would be acknowledged. God will be known as the One who controls history and destiny. The pain will yield some gain.

136

Was your prostitution not enough? You slaughtered my children and sacrificed them to the idols.

(Ezek. 16:20-21)

Scripture reading: Ezek. 16:1-31

The ingratitude and infidelity of Israel is described in a lengthy allegory. She was abandoned at birth, flung into a field, and left to die. She was rescued by the Lord, who watched over her growth until she became a beautiful queen.

A tragic descent into prostitution followed. Her "lewd conduct" reached its nadir in the sacrifice of her children to pagan gods.

The Lord declares, "I will bring upon you the blood vengeance of my wrath" (v. 38). Jerusalem will be handed over to her "lovers," to be stripped, stoned, and slashed to pieces. The sickening indictment closes, "Did you not add lewdness to all your other detestable practices?" (v. 43).

A woman who responds to love and care by lewdness, prostitution, and infanticide merits the severest punishment.

Is this just ancient history? Read your newspaper. Consider the children **"slaughtered"** and **"sacrificed"** in our society because their parents worship the idols of money, power, or sex. How can "enlightened" and "free" moderns, with so much blood on their hands, escape God's righteous judgment?

137

Will it thrive?

(Ezek. 17:9, 10)

Will he succeed?

(Ezek. 17:15)

Scripture reading: Ezek. 17:1-24

Nebuchadnezzar, after capturing Jerusalem, appointed Zedekiah to rule over its people. Zedekiah swore allegiance to Babylon, apparently in the name of the Lord. Though he was treated well by Nebuchadnezzar, Zedekiah sought a secret alliance with the Pharaoh of Egypt.

Jeremiah knew Egypt's history of broken treaties. Egypt would ravage, not protect, Judah. Furthermore, the oath taken in the Lord's name became His oath (v. 19). To violate the pact with Babylon, therefore, was to dishonor the Lord.

In the face of such duplicity, treachery, and blasphemy, can the vine thrive? Can Zedekiah succeed? No! He will be captured, his troops will be scattered, and his people will become exiles.

God will not play politics with anyone. No one can disgrace God's name without destroying himself. Sadly, too, no one can provoke his own ruin without bringing others down with him. The last thing Zedekiah saw, before being blinded by his captors, was the execution of his sons.

No one thrives, no one succeeds, who rebels against God.

138

What do you people mean by quoting this proverb about the land of Israel: "The fathers eat sour grapes, and the children's teeth are set on edge"?

(Ezek. 18:2)

Scripture reading: Ezek. 18:1-32

*E*zekiel's generation regarded themselves as victims, not as sinners. They blamed the woes of exile on the sins of their forefathers, for which God was now punishing them. Their proverb was as false as it was clever, and God corrects them with unsparing candor. They were being judged for their own sins.

Here the doctrine of individual responsibility is emphatically declared. "The soul who sins is the one who will die" (v. 4). A righteous father will not die for the sins of his wicked son. A righteous son will not die for the sins of his wicked father. The wicked man who repents and obeys God will live. The righteous man who turns from God to sin will die.

Guilt is nontransferable but not irremedial. The man who lives—spiritually—owes everything to the mercy of a forgiving God. The man who dies—spiritually—brings that judgment upon himself for refusing to repent and trust God.

139

Do I take any pleasure in the death of the wicked? declares the Sovereign Lord. Rather, am I not pleased when they turn from their ways and live?

(Ezek. 18:23)

Scripture reading: Ezek. 18:1-32

God makes two things crystal clear. One, that sin brings death; two, that He takes no pleasure in the sinner's death.

God delights in mercy. He is swift to forgive sins and to bestow life. He will do all He can to make forgiveness possible, but He cannot cease from being God. He must remain holy and just.

Sin can be forgiven or sin can be punished, but sin cannot be ignored. To expect God to ignore sin is to expect Him to be himself no longer.

Forgiveness is possible, but it is conditioned upon repentance—turning from sin to God. God justifies sinners, but He does not justify sinning. We either cease from sin and live, or we continue in sin and die. There is no third ground.

According to Jesus, heaven is filled with joy when one sinner repents (Luke 15:7, 10). And we who have repented and trusted in Jesus can testify that the sinner's heart is filled with joy also!

140

Why will you die, O house of Israel?

(Ezek. 18:31)

Scripture reading: Ezek. 18:21-32

*T*he Israelites were dying—alienated from God and exiled from home.

In a passage bristling with questions, God affirms the reason for that death, declares His displeasure in that death, and proclaims an escape route from that death.

The cause of death is sin, their own sin, not that of their ancestors. "If a righteous man turns from his righteousness and commits sin . . . will he live? . . . because of the sins he has committed, he will die" (v. 24).

God must punish sin, but He takes no pleasure in doing so. "Is my way unjust? Is it not your ways that are unjust?" (v. 25). Mercy often tempers justice, but mercy cannot negate justice. Unless the sinner repents, death must ensue.

There is an escape, not from justice, but from death. God identifies it with a single word—"Repent!" Turn from all sin, turn to God, and He will grant "a new heart and a new spirit" (v. 31).

God wills repentance, not death, for every sinner. "I take no pleasure in the death of anyone, declares the Sovereign Lord. Repent and live!" (v. 32).

He's talking to us.

141

Have you come to inquire of me?
As surely as I live,
I will not let you inquire of me,
declares the Sovereign Lord.

(Ezek. 20:3)

Scripture reading: Ezek. 20:1-38

*E*lders of Israel sat before Ezekiel awaiting an oracle from God. God refused to grant one. Instead, Ezekiel was told to "judge" them with a lesson in history that severely condemned them.

The lesson theme is the recurring apostasy of their fathers and the repeated mercy of God that pardoned and sustained them. Despite His fidelity to them, they were incurably attracted to the false gods and repulsive worship of surrounding nations. "Their hearts were devoted to their idols. Yet I looked on them with pity" (vv. 16-17).

Now the children are repeating and worsening the apostasy of the fathers. God says, "Will you defile yourselves the way your fathers did . . . ? Am I to let you inquire of me, O house of Israel?" (vv. 30-31). Having failed to learn from history, they will now be judged "with outpoured wrath" (v. 33).

Even so, God will temper justice with mercy. The exiles are promised a new Exodus. A remnant purged of idolatry will be restored, and their worship will be accepted. By judgment and grace God vindicates His name, His holiness.

142

If you despise the rod, will it not happen?

(Ezek. 21:13, NRSV)

Scripture reading: Ezek. 21:8-17

*T*he rod was used to chasten in order to reform behavior, thus promoting truer fellowship with God, and averting worse punishment for sin.

The rod had failed, not because God unwisely employed it, but because Israel stubbornly despised it. The people were intractably idolatrous.

The sword would now replace the rod, and great slaughter would result. Brandishing a sword, Ezekiel acted out his message, furiously slashing the air right and left.

The sword is not for correction but for destruction after correction has been refused. God will clap His hands to summon a slayer—Babylon—and clap them again to halt the destruction when justice has been served.

We may dislike this portrait of God, but that's because we are soft on sin. We would sacrifice divine justice to human pleasure. God's love is tougher and truer.

Despise the rod, expect the sword. Sin must be dealt with one way or the other.

143

Will you judge this city of bloodshed?

(Ezek. 22:2)

Scripture reading: Ezek. 22:1-12

*T*he prophet was to "judge" the bloody city by listing her evils and describing her punishment. In doing so, he spoke for God.

He catalogs religious, political, personal, and social sins. Nothing has been regarded as sacred. No one's person or property have been safe from human predators. Right has been defined by might. The strong have cruelly exploited the weak. God has been forgotten in the very city where He graciously consented to put His name.

Those who abused their power and corrupted the city will now be judged by a greater power. The city will be ravished and its people captured by an enemy nation.

God derides the boasted power of the city with a single question: "Will your courage endure or your hands be strong in the day I deal with you?" (v. 14). Against Him the strongest must fall.

The sins named in Ezekiel's indictment are occurring in our cities daily. Can we escape judgment? Only if we repent. The unchanging God is at once our Threat and our Hope.

144

Son of man,
will you judge Oholah and Oholibah?

(Ezek. 23:36)

Scripture reading: Ezek. 23:1-49

Oholah and Oholibah were allegorical names for the nations of Israel and Judah. Ezekiel was to "judge" them by denouncing their sins and announcing their punishment.

The specific indictment focuses on idolatry, which led in turn to every kind of evil. Adopting pagan gods meant also adopting pagan morals.

The sister nations are depicted as unfaithful wives of God. Idolatry is pictured as adultery. The brazen defiance of the two nations is accented in a single sentence: "On the very day they sacrificed their children to their idols, they entered my sanctuary and desecrated it" (v. 39).

Their presence in God's house defiled it. The worship of those who had practiced human sacrifice at pagan altars slandered the Holy One.

Judgment was determined. Invaders would terrorize and plunder both guilty kingdoms. Thousands would be slaughtered, and survivors would be deported. Then the smitten nations would know that God is the Sovereign Lord.

They could have learned from mercy what they would learn from justice. A school of rebels will find their tuition terribly expensive.

145

*Will not the coastlands tremble
at the sound of your fall,
when the wounded groan and
the slaughter takes place in you?*

(Ezek. 26:15)

Scripture reading: Ezek. 26:1-21

*A*ncient Tyre was renowned for beauty and wealth—
and arrogance. She forged commercial monopolies
in hope of becoming the greatest maritime power on earth.
Her fleets were the jewels of the Mediterranean, piling up
riches with every voyage. In her pride she even declared
herself a god (28:9).

Tyre rejoiced when Jerusalem was destroyed. A rival
was out of business; her own wealth would now increase.

Then God spoke. "I am against you, O Tyre, and I will
bring many nations against you, like the sea casting up its
waves" (v. 3).

A tidal wave of judgment would reduce Tyre's island
fortress to a bare rock on which fishermen would dry their
nets. The city would be demolished and disappear beneath
the sea, never to rise again.

And that is what happened. Any nation that trades
blows with God will be knocked out. Any person likewise.
God humbles the proud.

146

Will you then say, "I am a god," in the presence of those who kill you?

(Ezek. 28:9)

Scripture reading: Ezek. 28:1-10

The ruler of Tyre boasted, "I am a god; I sit on the throne of a god" (v. 2).

God rejoined, "You are a man" (v. 2). The tyrant's wisdom and power are admitted, but the admission is followed by an announcement of his defeat by invaders. "They will bring you down to the pit, and you will die a violent death" (v. 8). The god claims will be silenced by judgment.

A man claiming to be a god is not unique in history. Many rulers have made that boast in words or deeds. Death savagely stripped the mask from each pretender, exposing their frailty and mortality.

No man rises too high for God to bring low. No man accumulates so much wealth that God cannot bankrupt him. Nor does any nation.

The human "I am," contradicted by the divine "You are," is an empty boast inviting disaster. Only fools make it; only fools believe it. God became Man to save us. Men become gods and destroy themselves.

147

Who can be compared with you in majesty?

(Ezek. 31:2)

Scripture reading: Ezek. 31:1-18

God directs the question above to "Pharaoh king of Egypt and to his hordes." They would be quick to answer, "No one."

God agreed. A superpower had developed along the Nile, outstripping the other nations in political, commercial, and martial strength.

Yes, like Assyria before it, Egypt now towered above other nations as a majestic cedar rises grandly above the other trees of the forest. But Assyria had been rejected by God, cut down and left to rot.

"You are next," God is saying to Egypt and its ruler. He repeats the question about their peerless splendor and adds, "Yet you, too, will be brought down" (v. 18). Proud Egyptians will lie beside supposed "inferiors" in death. Death democratizes. All the trees, including the majestic cedar, descend at last into Sheol.

God can provide an ax to fell the loftiest of trees. Those who proudly seek to usurp His glory cannot escape His wrath. Great or small, nations and persons rebel against Him, only to meet destruction.

148

Say to them,
"Are you more favored than others?"

(Ezek. 32:19)

Scripture reading: Ezek. 32:17-21

*P*haraoh esteemed himself "a lion among the nations" (v. 2). He was a river monster roiling the waters as he thrashed about. God decreed that he would be netted and hauled to his death by a horde from Babylon.

Egypt's number one deity was Re, the sun god. God declared that Egypt would be filled with darkness.

Thus God would triumph over the gods of Egypt and bring down their earthly representative. Pharaoh and his hordes would not be favored above others. They would not escape the pit into which other tyrants and armies had descended. There, defeated and deflated, they would "bear their shame" who had boasted of their might (v. 24).

In judgment, God would teach them that He is Lord. Had not sin blinded them, they could have learned that lesson in a happier school at a lower tuition.

Death, like God, is no respecter of persons. Worms feast gladly upon great and small. Hell opens widely for rich and poor. Anyone who thinks he can displace or outwit God has a rude awakening coming.

149

Why will you die, O house of Israel?

(Ezek. 33:11)

Scripture reading: Ezek. 33:1-20

*D*eath is more than loss of physical life. It is loss of life spiritually and eternally.

The prophet was a watchman giving warning. His message was blunt—repent or perish. Centuries later Jesus would voice the same alternative (Luke 13:3, 5). The identical warning is raised today by honest preachers.

"I will judge each of you according to his own ways," declared the Lord (v. 20). Our destiny is determined by choosing the ways of God or the ways of sin. We turn from sin to God and live, or we turn from God to sin and die.

Occasional lapses into sin by one who had turned to God is not the burden of this passage. The metaphor is "way"—a continuing journey, not an infrequent misstep.

God takes no pleasure in the death of the wicked, but He does sentence the wicked to death. He is swift to forgive all who repent. He is sure to punish all who do not repent.

Why will you die . . . ? The answer to God's question is simply this, "Because you refuse to repent." Divine grace has made every person's repentance possible. Only one's deliberate refusal of grace makes destruction inevitable.

The ball is in your court!

150

Should you then possess the land?

(Ezek. 33:25, 26)

Scripture reading: Ezek. 33:21-33

*J*ust before Jerusalem fell, the question shown was put twice to the fellow exiles of Ezekiel.

God brought Israel into the Promised Land as His covenant people. Breaking the covenant had become their ingrained habit. Should they continue, then, to possess the land?

Canaan was an undeserved gift, but not an unconditioned gift. As early as the promise was made, the warnings were also given. The land could be forfeited by disobedience to the covenant stipulations.

The prophet's messages rolled from the people's hearts like rain from a steep roof. They were merely spectators being entertained, who then turned away to repeat their deliberate and detestable sins.

God keeps His covenant, both its blessings and its cursings. When judgment comes, they will know that a prophet, not an entertainer, has been in their midst.

The people's choice is to obey or to reject God's word. The preacher's choice is to prophesy or to entertain. One prophet said, "While I was musing the fire burned" (Ps. 39:3, KJV). One preacher said, "While I was amusing the fire went out."

151

Should not shepherds take care of the flock?

(Ezek. 34:2)

Scripture reading: Ezek. 34:1-16

*I*srael was a flock, and its rulers were shepherds. Kings and priests, however, proved to be false shepherds. To satisfy their vanity and greed, they exploited and destroyed the flock. They did not seek the lost, tend the hurt, feed the weak, or teach the strong. Consequently, the flock was scattered and helpless before its enemies.

God pledges to oppose and remove the shepherds. In a splendid promise He said, "I myself will search for my sheep and look after them" (v. 11). Again, "I will shepherd the flock with justice" (v. 16). Abundant grace and adequate protection will be given to a restored Israel.

Divine shepherding reached its ultimate expression in Jesus Christ, who came "to seek and to save what was lost" (Luke 19:10). Jesus said, "I am the good shepherd. The good shepherd lays down his life for the sheep" (John 10:11). The evil shepherds sacrificed the flock to themselves. The Good Shepherd sacrificed himself for the flock.

Is it not enough for you to feed on the good pasture? Must you also trample the rest of your pasture with your feet? Is it not enough for you to drink clear water? Must you also muddy the rest with your feet? Must my flock feed on what you have trampled and drink what you have muddied with your feet?

(Ezek. 34:18-19)

Scripture reading: Ezek. 34:17-31

The first sheep to reach high grass eat their fill but trample the pasture as they do. The first sheep to reach a clear stream drink their fill but leave the stream muddy. Heartless rulers in Israel used brute force to insure their own interests, butting and shoving and plundering the weak (v. 21).

God, the new and true Shepherd, pledges to bring judgment against their greed and violence. He will judge between "rams and goats," between "the fat . . . and the lean" (vv. 17, 20).

Concentration of wealth in the hands of a few, while masses are deprived and oppressed, offends God. It cannot be justified by specious appeals to some "natural law" dubbed "survival of the fittest."

Wealth and power gained and used by exploiting the defenseless will bring a person down to hell as sure as God is God.

153

Son of man, can these bones live?

(Ezek. 37:3)

Scripture reading: Ezek. 37:1-14

*B*y the Spirit" Ezekiel was transported to a valley filled with human bones, very many and "very dry" (vv. 1, 2). It was like Sunday morning in a large modern church.

"Can these bones live?" challenged God. The prophet wisely answered, "You alone know."

At God's command Ezekiel prophesied to the bones—"You will come to life" (vv. 7, 6). The word of the Lord brought the bones together, and skeletons were formed. Next they were clothed with sinew and flesh, and finally they were given breath. As the prophet watched, they came to life and stood up—"a vast army" (v. 10).

God explained the vision. Israel would have a national resurrection. She would be released from captivity and restored to her homeland. "I will put my Spirit in you and you will live," the Almighty promised (v. 14).

By the power of God's Word and Spirit the dead can live. This truth is often demonstrated in the conversion of sinners and the revival of churches.

154

In that day, when my people Israel are living in safety, will you not take notice of it? . . . Are you not the one I spoke of in former days by my servants the prophets of Israel?

(Ezek. 38:14, 17)

Scripture reading: Ezek. 38:1-23

*I*n this passage, notoriously difficult to interpret, a coalition of warriors under the command of a prince named Gog strikes at Israel, intending to loot the "unwalled villages" of a "peaceful and unsuspecting people" (v. 11).

Ezekiel prophesies against Gog. The raiders will discover to their grief that the apparently helpless people were guarded by the Lord himself.

Utilizing natural forces, the Lord will utterly destroy the marauders. Gog will find his grave in Israel. Burial of all the dead will take seven months. Israel will plunder the plunderers and loot the looters, totally reversing Gog's "evil scheme" (v. 10).

The Lord saw it coming in "former days," and His prophets spoke of it (v. 17). He brought these barbarians against Israel in order to display His greatness and holiness. The invaders were His unwitting tools.

Wonderful Watchman! He is never surprised, never defeated. In Him alone is the security of His people.

155

Son of man, do you see this?

(Ezek. 47:6)

Scripture reading: Ezek. 47:1-12

*E*zekiel's vision of the restored Temple has a dramatic climax. From the Temple issues a stream of water, growing from a trickle to a torrent. Lengthening and deepening, it flows into and transforms the Dead Sea.

The river's source is the holy of holies—in short, God. "Where the river flows everything will live" (v. 9). A once desolate and arid region will become groves of trees whose fruit will feed and heal the nations.

God's presence and power is the source of renewal and life. Ultimately, He undoes the damage and pollution of centuries. He brings the dead to life.

In a sense, that life-giving and life-sustaining stream is already flowing from Calvary. There Jesus provided renewal, cleansing, and healing for the dry, polluted, and fruitless existence of sinners.

Will the prophet's vision have a literal fulfillment? I must leave that with God. Meanwhile, I plunge into the river of life that is already in motion and eternally efficacious!

156

The Israelites are stubborn,
like a stubborn heifer.
How then can the Lord pasture them
like lambs in a meadow?

(Hos. 4:16)

Scripture reading: Hos. 4:1-19

*I*srael is charged with adultery and prostitution, and Judah is warned against her shameful example. Though swearing by the living God, Israel flocked to pagan rites, sinking to the abysmal level of temple prostitution (v. 14).

When charged with sin and called to repent, the rebels persisted in their idolatry. They were as stubborn as a balky heifer.

Stubborn heifers cannot be handled like gentle lambs. A broad pasture is not the answer. Increasing their blessings will not induce repentance. The time has come for judgment: "A whirlwind will sweep them away" (v. 19).

Hosea's message to Judah—and to us—is clear. Separation is vital to holiness. "Ephraim is joined to idols; leave him alone!" (v. 17). Share the sins of the impenitent, and you must also share their punishment.

The Lord wants His people in the world but not of the world.

157

What can I do with you, Ephraim? What can I do with you, Judah? Your love is like the morning mist, like the early dew that disappears.

(Hos. 6:4)

Scripture reading: Hos. 6:1-11

God's people have become apostates threatened with judgment. They are urged to return to Him, the only source of healing and life.

They presume upon His help. They take Him for granted, as they do sunrise in the morning and rainfall in the spring (vv. 1-3).

But God sees past praying lips to lying hearts, and He rejects their worship. Their sacrifices are belied by continuing disloyalty to Him and continuing crimes against others (vv. 6-10).

Like a frustrated father whose kindness has failed to correct a wayward son, the Lord laments, **"What can I do with you . . . ?"** They have left Him one alternative: a judgment that flashes like lightning.

The prophets' unheeded warnings will now be actuated. Their refusal to repent is a seed of rebellion from which a bitter harvest will be reaped (v. 11). They have spurned healing; they will experience hell.

158

How long will they be incapable of purity?

(Hos. 8:5)

Scripture reading: Hos. 8:1-10

God's people were affirming Him with their lips but denying Him in their lives. They broke His covenant and transgressed His law (v. 1). They chose their rulers without consulting Him. They made false gods in defiance of the true God.

His patience stretched thin, God asks, **"How long . . . ?"** How long before the nation truly worships God? How long before its character and behavior are reformed? The sad truth is, not until they endure a refining judgment.

The trumpet sounds an alarm. A bird of prey hovers above the house of God. A whirlwind of judgment approaches (vv. 1, 7).

God's anger is burning against them. Their metal gods and treasonous leaders will prove highly combustible. The nation that turned from a merciful Benefactor will waste away under a foreign oppressor (vv. 6, 10).

"Sow the wind and reap the whirlwind" (v. 7). You cannot challenge the sovereignty of God without inviting your own destruction.

159

Since the days of Gibeah, you have sinned,
O Israel, and there you have remained.
Did not war overtake the evildoers in Gibeah?

(Hos. 10:9)

Scripture reading: Hos. 10:1-15

Gibeah was the home of Saul, Israel's first king. The monarchy in Israel began as a rejection of God. It expressed loss of confidence in His provision of charismatic leadership for the nation.

Israel wanted to be like other nations, preferring the wisdom of kings to that of God. She wanted foreign policy dictated by a king, not priests and prophets. God consented to the monarchy but warned the people of its harsh future consequences (1 Samuel 8).

A history of broken alliances and bloody conflicts had confirmed God's warnings. Few godly kings had ruled, and the nation became increasingly idolatrous and immoral. Now Hosea predicts the destruction of the monarchy and the extinction of the nation.

Israel tried to appease pagan rulers at the cost of offending God. Now the dance is ending, and it's time to pay the fiddler. "When I please," God says, "I will punish them" (v. 10). In His own time and place and manner God will always bring judgment upon sin.

160

Will they not return to Egypt and will not Assyria rule over them because they refuse to repent?

(Hos. 11:5)

Scripture reading: Hos. 11:1-7

God's love for Israel defies human understanding. Israel was His son, called from bondage to freedom. He made a covenant to secure and supply His people, and they pledged to honor and obey Him.

His care was constant and tender, but Israel proved to be ungrateful and disloyal. They stubbornly sacrificed to pagan gods, attributing to those grotesque and lifeless images the mercies received from the living God.

God taught His son to walk—and the son walked away from his Father! Distance increased as idolatry worsened.

Now, God says, the nation that would not return to Him will return to bondage, this time in Assyria.

When God called to them, they kept walking away. Now, when they call on Him, He will not spare them from this judgment. He may not be loved and honored, but neither will He be used and discarded.

We never get rid of God. He is either Savior or Judge.

161

How can I give you up, Ephraim?
How can I hand you over, Israel?

(Hos. 11:8)

Scripture reading: Hos. 11:1-11

When you read of the infidelity and immorality of Israel, you are tempted to ask, "How can He *not* give them up?" She has betrayal in her heart and blood on her hands. Why not divorce her once and for all?

Here's the answer: "I am God, and not man—the Holy One among you" (v. 9). He is God, and "God is love" (1 John 4:8, 16), and love reluctantly punishes but readily pardons. As Roy Hunnicutt has written, "There is a wrath in God's love and a love in God's wrath." If that creates tension in our thinking, imagine the tension in God's heart.

Dr. James McCord, of Princeton Seminary, once told a group of professors, "My favorite heresy is Patripassianism." That the Father suffers with His children may be heresy to those whose God is a philosophical abstraction, but not to those whose God is the Father to whom the Bible bears witness—a Person whose love cannot be quenched even by our sins.

He could not give them up. He would punish them but not disown them. For all who chose to accept it, there was a way back to Him.

Where is your king, that he may save you?
Where are your rulers in all your towns,
of whom you said,
"Give me a king and princes"?

(Hos. 13:10)

Scripture reading: Hos. 13:1-13

God ruled Israel, but they clamored for an earthly king. They wanted to be like other nations. The monarchy, they believed, would result in national stability and political power. Instead, bad rulers led them into apostasy. Now they are as unstable as mist, chaff, and smoke (vv. 1-3).

The Lord who had saved them was now going to destroy them. He was coming against them like an angry bear or a hungry lion (vv. 4-9). Who could stop Him? Scornfully He asks, **"Where is your king, that he may save you?"**

They will languish in exile, and their king will be the captive servant of their heathen oppressor. They will learn the hard way that the Lord alone is God and Savior.

Whom the Lord cannot rule He overrules. "In my anger I gave you a king, and in my wrath I took him away" (v. 11). Only the Lord is indispensable to the security and prosperity of His people. That is as true of the modern Christian as it was of ancient Israel.

163

Where, O death, are your plagues?
Where, O grave, is your destruction?

(Hos. 13:14)

Scripture reading: Hos. 13:9-16

*I*n the *New International Version* the questions listed above
follow promises: "I will ransom them from the power
of the grave; I will redeem them from death." God seems
to be taunting death and Sheol as powers inferior to His
own.

Paul gives the passage this positive meaning in 1 Cor.
15:55, where he exults in the conquest of death through the
resurrection of Christ. He quotes the passage from the Sep-
tuagint, an ancient Greek translation of the Old Testament.

However, the Hebrew text of verse 14*a* can be rendered as questions, not affirmations. Thus the *Revised Standard Version* reads: "Shall I ransom them from the power of
Sheol? Shall I redeem them from Death?" God then summons death and Sheol to serve as instruments of His judgment upon His apostate people. "I will have no compassion" (v. 14).

In either case, the Lord is in control. Whether He is
taunting their impotence or enlisting their service, death
and Sheol obey Him. He is Lord of life and death and eternity!

164

O Ephraim,
what more have I to do with idols?

(Hos. 14:8)

Scripture reading: Hos. 14:1-9

*T*he question given sounds awkward. The marginal reading seems helpful: "What more has Ephraim to do with idols?"

The context promises restoration from captivity. When the people repent (vv. 1-3), God will forgive, restore, and heal. These gifts of love will allow His people to flourish again in their own land.

If we read "I," the answer is God has nothing to do with idols except to condemn and destroy them. This is all He ever had to do with them. Idols do not form a peer group for Him. He alone is God. They have no real existence. His judgment is their defeat.

If we read "Ephraim," the answer is still nothing. Israel, cured of idolatry and grateful for Exodus II, which restores them to their homeland, will serve the Lord only, and He will make them fruitful.

Any person's happiest day occurs when he or she renounces all idols and turns wholeheartedly to the true God and Savior.

Has anything like this ever happened in your days or in the days of your forefathers?

(Joel 1:2)

Scripture reading: Joel 1:1-15

*A*n enormous horde of voracious locusts had stripped the land of all produce and left the stunned population to face famine. Farmers wailed and priests mourned over the ruined country.

Swarms of locusts were not rare in the Mideast, but this one was unprecedented for size and damage. Search personal memory and national history, the prophet declares, and you will find no parallel to this catastrophe.

These locusts are depicted by Joel as instruments of divine judgment upon the apostate kingdom of Judah. They formed an army, under the command of God, that darkened and destroyed the land.

The invasion and destruction that he describes in the graphic details of an eyewitness are a prelude to the coming day of the Lord. The Lord is striding forward to meet the nations in swift, terrible, and righteous judgment.

That judgment will begin at His house, with His people, and extend to all nations. None can prevent it; none can escape it.

166

Now what have you against me,
O Tyre and Sidon
and all you regions of Philistia?
Are you repaying me for something
I have done?

(Joel 3:4)

Scripture reading: Joel 3:4-8

*L*awsuit metaphors are a common prophetic device. Here God appears before Phoenicia and Philistia, first as an accuser bringing charges, then as a judge pronouncing sentence.

When Jerusalem fell, these people looted the Temple. Further, and worse, they took Israelites captive and sold them as slaves to distant nations.

Israel was God's possession, His special treasure. The Temple was His house, its furnishings His property. In defying His ownership, they challenged His rights and power. They not only had stolen things and wronged people but had blasphemed God.

Now they would learn that life has a boomerang effect. What you do is done to you. What you sow you reap. "I will swiftly and speedily return on your own heads what you have done" (v. 4). Their lands would be desolated, their treasures confiscated, their people enslaved. To quote a current adage, "What goes around comes around."

167

Is this not true, people of Israel?

(Amos 2:11)

Scripture reading: Amos 2:6-16

*A*mos had been lambasting the sins and proclaiming the judgment of other nations. Hearers alert to geography would be getting uneasy, for each nation named was closer to Israel than those before.

Then, sure enough, wham! "For three sins of Israel, even for four, I will not turn back my wrath" (v. 6). Israel's sins were listed, and God's mercies to them were recounted. Against this backdrop of mercy their sins stood out as less excusable and more punishable than those of pagan neighbors.

God demanded admission of the truth—**"Is this not true, people of Israel?"**

Sooner or later every nation and every person will confess their sins, admit their guilt, and take their punishment. "Now then," says God, "I will crush you" (v. 13). From His appointed justice none can escape, not the swiftest, not the strongest, not the bravest! In the words of an old song, "You can't do wrong and get by."

168

Did you bring me sacrifices and offerings forty years in the desert, O house of Israel?

(Amos 5:25)

Scripture reading: Amos 5:18-27

A prophetic "woe" is addressed to those who longed for the day of the Lord, vainly supposing that Israel would be spared the judgments that would then fall upon other nations. Not so, says Amos. "That day will be darkness, not light" (v. 18).

Israel's worship would not save her. Her gatherings, sacrifices, and music were negated by the injustice and unrighteousness that corrupted her daily life.

The answer to God's question in verse 25 is no. During those desert years, Israel lacked the resources and opportunity to offer the sacrifices and observe the rituals that were later practiced under the Law. Nevertheless, God was in their midst, accessible to those who sought communion with Him. Essential to fellowship with Him is justice and obedience, not sacrifices and rituals.

Where justice is absent from human relationships, another bleeding animal, another smoking altar, another solemn hymn serve only to increase hypocrisy and therefore to insure punishment. That's something to ponder in our Sunday gatherings, is it not?

169

What do you see, Amos?

(Amos 7:8)

Scripture reading: Amos 7:1-9

*T*he question given was easy to answer. The prophet saw the Lord standing by a wall with a plumb line in His hand.

God was setting a plumb line in the midst of Israel—the plumb line of His demand for justice and righteousness. It would expose the crookedness of the nation and make their judgment inevitable.

Centers of worship would be destroyed as a judgment on hypocrisy. The ruling dynasty would be toppled as a judgment on corrupt leadership.

Earlier, visions of swarming locusts and devouring flames had wrung prayers of intercession from the prophet (vv. 1-6). God "relented" and spared His people from deserved ruin.

Now Amos does not intercede. It's too late to pray. The sword of justice has been unsheathed, and God will no longer spare His disloyal people. God's love is unfailing, but human hearts can become so hardened by sin that repentance is impossible. Then judgment becomes inevitable.

170

What do you see, Amos?

(Amos 8:2)

Scripture reading: Amos 8:1-14

*T*he prophet answers the question shown, "A basket of ripe fruit." The meaning was obvious and alarming. Israel was ripe for judgment. God would "spare them no longer" (v. 2).

"In that day . . ." The phrase occurs three times here, introducing dire prophecies of slaughter, sorrow, and silence.

Slaughter! "Many, many bodies—flung everywhere!" (v. 3).

Sorrow! "I will turn your religious feasts into mourning" (v. 10). Sobbing will replace singing.

Silence! "I will send a famine . . . a famine of hearing the words of the Lord" (v. 11).

The greedy had exploited, cheated, and sold the needy. Then they dared to enter God's house to sing, pray, and offer sacrifices. Now they will dress in sackcloth, tremble before an angry God, and mourn like parents who have buried their only son. The Word of God—source of light and hope and joy—will not be found.

This passage of Scripture makes an honest person tremble for the future of our own nation!

171

Are not you Israelites the same to me as the Cushites?

(Amos 9:7)

Scripture reading: Amos 9:1-15

Within Israel were men who scoffed at the message of judgment. "Disaster will not overtake . . . us" was their smug reply to the prophet's warnings (v. 10). They interpreted election as privilege, not as obligation. They were God's chosen people, and He would never destroy them.

Wrong! The Lord declares that He is sovereign of all nations, and none are exempt from judgment upon their sins, not even Israel. Any nation that defies His will becomes the architect of its own destruction.

He will not totally destroy Israel, however. A remnant will survive the Exile and return to the homeland, to rebuild and inhabit its ruined cities. The Exile will be a sifting process. The grain will be preserved, and the trash will be eliminated.

Far beyond the prophet's vision, the remnant was finally reduced to a lonely figure on a Roman cross—Jesus, the Son of God. From Him would spring a new covenant, a new Israel, a new Jerusalem.

172

Have you any right to be angry?

(Jonah 4:4)

Scripture reading: Jonah 1:1—4:11

God spared Nineveh and Jonah pouted. He wanted the pagan city destroyed, thus removing a threat to Israel's well-being.

He prayed to die. Living as an instrument of divine mercy to Gentiles galled him. God didn't kill him but attempted something harder—the reeducation of a bigot.

A vine was provided to shelter the prophet's head, and Jonah was happy for the comfort. A worm killed the vine, and the blazing sun and blasting wind made Jonah so miserable that he prayed again to die.

"Do you have a right to be angry about the vine?" God asked. "Angry enough to die," was the churlish answer (v. 9). God gently rebuked his mean, jingoistic spirit. Jonah wanted a vine to live but a city to die. God valued people above all creatures: "Should I not be concerned about that great city?" (v. 11).

What reflects our own attitude—the bigoted spirit of Jonah or the pitying love of God? Are we more concerned for things that provide our comfort than for lost people whose only hope is God's mercy?

173

Do not my words do good to him whose ways are upright?

(Mic. 2:7)

Scripture reading: Mic. 2:1-11

*F*alse prophets tried to muzzle Micah. Claiming covenant promises but ignoring covenant warnings, they portrayed God as the obligated Protector of apostate Israel.

Their "peace and prosperity" message pleased the greedy landowners who enlarged vast estates by brutal eviction of widows and orphans from their homes. They put out the welcome mat to prophets who would lie and deceive as their partners in crime.

Micah preached the whole truth, blessings and cursings, promises and threats. God's words would hurt only those who rebelled against Him. The whole truth was beneficial to the upright.

As for the land barons, they had evicted the helpless, and now God would evict them. They would perish in exile, but God would bring back a faithful remnant to rebuild the wasted homeland.

You can hear hireling prophets and their gospel of material prosperity any day on radio and television. We need some Micahs whose mouths are not for rent.

174

My people, what have I done to you?
How have I burdened you?

(Mic. 6:3)

Scripture reading: Mic. 6:1-8

A lawsuit is in progress—*The Lord vs. Israel.*
"What have I done?" the Plaintiff asks. What action of Mine justifies your disloyalty and rebellion? God has done nothing to warrant their breach of covenant. He has done everything to merit their fidelity.

He brought them up from Egypt into Canaan, from bondage to freedom. Other examples of saving mercy abound in their history. They have no defense.

What shall we do? Let's get the trial over with. We plead guilty; now what will pacify God? Does He want more and better sacrifices? Does He want rivers of oil? We will even sacrifice our firstborn sons as offerings to Him. Their response is saturated with sarcasm.

What God requires was right there in the confession of faith they made and in the covenant demands they knew. "Act justly . . . love mercy . . . walk humbly with your God" (v. 8). All life's relationship to God and people must be governed by right attitudes and actions, those that spring from genuine love for God and neighbor. Apart from this, intensified religion only brings intensified guilt.

175

Am I still to forget, O wicked house,
your ill-gotten treasures and the short ephah,
which is accursed? Shall I acquit a man
with dishonest scales,
with a bag of false weights?

(Mic. 6:10-11)

Scripture reading: Mic. 6:9-16

*T*he ax of judgment now gashes the world of commerce. God is angry with greedy merchants who resort to violence and deception to fatten their purses.

His covenant with Israel demanded honest dealing and accurate weights and measures. With no one to inspect and regulate commerce, the public was helplessly bullied and bilked by unscrupulous dealers.

The covenant included curses upon dishonest businessmen. God is going to enforce those curses. The process of judgment has begun.

Their labors will be wasted, their investments will be destroyed, for heartless invaders will decimate the people and plunder their produce. Those once admired as clever and successful will become objects of contempt and ridicule. Tributes will give place to taunts as wealthy merchants go into exile as bankrupts.

God's judgment begins at His house, but it doesn't stop short of the marketplace. White-collar criminals, beware!

Will not all of them taunt him
with ridicule and scorn, saying,
"Woe to him who piles up stolen goods
and makes himself wealthy by extortion!
How long must this go on?"
Will not your debtors suddenly arise?
Will they not wake up and make you tremble?

(Hab. 2:6-7)

Scripture reading: Hab. 2:1-8

Chaldea had sacked and enslaved other nations to create its vast wealth. The exiles in Chaldea from the looted nations are apparently helpless now, but they are destined to revolt against and overcome their oppressors in the future. "How long" will become "now."

Five "woes" are spoken against the swaggering bully. Their overall message is, "You will get from others what you have dished out to them." The plunderer will be plundered, the captor will be captured, the destroyer will be destroyed.

The Bible never wearies of proclaiming life's boomerang effect. The treatment accorded others comes back in kind. God rules a moral universe. However long delayed, the day of judgment comes, and accounts are squared. "God is not mocked"—we reap what we sow (Gal. 6:7, KJV). No one can really break the law of the harvest, but many have been broken by it.

177

Has not the Lord Almighty determined that the people's labor is only fuel for the fire, that the nations exhaust themselves for nothing?

(Hab. 2:13)

Scripture reading: Hab. 2:9-14

God sends a message to the conqueror who builds his capital city with blood—with confiscated materials and slave laborers from plundered nations.

The proud memorials being erected will become fuel for the fire. The Lord has decreed it! The conqueror will be conquered, and his city will be torched. The buildings that now stand as monuments to the pride and power of evil men will become ash piles, mute testimonies to the righteous judgment of the Lord.

Beyond the destruction of arrogant, enslaving nations will arise the kingdom of God, destined to overspread the whole world. Knowledge of the glory of God will fill the earth as waters cover the ocean floors. In that Kingdom all will be free, all will be filled, all will be fulfilled. The world will know at last how holy and happy the Creator meant life on earth to be.

This is no wistful utopia, no insubstantial dream stuff of weary slaves. This has been *determined* by the Lord. It will be!

178

Of what value is an idol,
since a man has carved it?
Or an image that teaches lies? . . .
Can it give guidance?

(Hab. 2:18-19)

Scripture reading: Hab. 2:18-20

*H*abakkuk's last "woe" is directed against idolatry: "Woe to him who says to wood, 'Come to life!' Or to lifeless stone, 'Wake up!'" (v. 19).

"Lifeless" says it all. The gilded gods of wood and stone and metal might look impressive, but having no life, they could neither give life nor save life.

What can be more futile than shouting at, or praying to, an unseeing, unhearing, unspeaking *thing* that cannot respond? Man prostrate before the work of his own hands, seeking guidance from mindless matter, is doomed to frustration and failure.

In the sharpest contrast imaginable, Habakkuk exclaims, "But the Lord is in his holy temple; let all the earth be silent before him" (v. 20). Hush your mouth and hold your breath—the Lord is preparing judgment against all idols and all idolaters. He is the true God who sees, hears, speaks, and acts to determine the outcome of history.

Oh, that we can say of Him, "*My* Lord and *my* God!" (John 20:28, italics added).

Is it a time for you yourselves to be living in your paneled houses, while this house remains a ruin? . . . What you brought home, I blew away. Why? . . . Because of my house, which remains a ruin, while each of you is busy with his own house.

(Hag. 1:4, 9)

Scripture reading: Hag. 1:1-11

N ot yet," said the people when the prophet urged them to rebuild the Temple. They mean to do it, but later on. Right now they are too busy with their own houses, lands, and crops. Times are hard and food is scarce. Just getting by is their priority.

No, says the Lord. My neglected house is the very reason for your misfortune. *I* blow away what you bring home. *I* withhold the rains, and your crops fail. Your economic plight is a judgment upon your false priorities.

The true center of human life is the worship of God. Unless the center holds, all life will fall apart. God's house was the symbol of His glory, His presence with, and power over, His people. Rebuild the Temple, restore the glory, and the result will be *shalom*—total well-being.

Self at the center of life is idolatrous and destructive. God at the center hallows and heals all other relationships.

*Who of you is left who saw this house
in its former glory? How does it look to you
now? Does it not seem to you like nothing?*

(Hag. 2:3)

Scripture reading: Hag. 2:1-9

Solomon's Temple had been glorious in appearance. The wealth of material and craftsmen at his disposal assured the grandeur of the building.

By comparison, the rebuilt Temple looked like "nothing." No matter, says the Lord. The true glory of the Temple is His presence, with His people before Him in sincere worship. "I will fill this house with glory," He promises (v. 7).

The treasures of nations will flow into it. *Shalom* will flow out from it, that spiritual and material well-being that is His gift to an obedient people.

Therefore, "Be strong . . . and work," the Lord commands the rulers, priests, and commoners—"I am with you" (v. 4).

His presence is the source of present courage and future blessing. He is with those who put Him at the center of life. All others live on the margins, chronically unhappy and ultimately destroyed. He *is* life. His presence is life's glory; His absence is life's misery.

181

Is there yet any seed left in the barn?

(Hag. 2:19)

Scripture reading: Hag. 2:10-19

*T*he people had refused to put God first. They had disobeyed the prophetic commands to rebuild the Temple. Consequently, the Lord had struck their fields with "blight, mildew, and hail" (v. 17).

Now that the Temple was being restored, things would be different. The vines would flourish and the groves would be fruitful. **"Is there yet any seed left in the barn?"** Plant it, and expect it to be productive. God promises, "From this day on I will bless you" (v. 19).

The fault had not been in the seed but in the sower. The people had been self-centered, not God-centered. Now giving Him priority over all else, they could count on His blessing. The same kind of seed would now bring forth a different measure of harvest.

Temple and worship do not automatically confer blessing, otherwise the Exile would never have occurred. God's true house is His people's hearts. When He abides there, the Temple is a channel of blessing to all of life, including fields and crops.

Who has priority in your life?

182

Where are your forefathers now?
And the prophets, do they live forever?
But did not my words and my decrees,
which I commanded my servants
the prophets, overtake your forefathers?

(Zech 1:5-6)

Scripture reading: Zech. 1:1-6

*R*eturn to me, . . . and I will return to you," the Lord says, merging command and promise (v. 3).

Only His presence satisfies the human heart, but He does not force himself upon us. He will not dwell where He is not welcome as Lord of one's whole life.

The fathers had made Him marginal, not central. As a result they were dominated by sin and devastated by judgment.

Don't be like your fathers, He is saying. They stopped their ears and steeled their hearts against the word I sent to them by the prophets. They are gone now, as are the prophets who tried to help them, but My Word abides. No one can escape My Word. It overtakes you, to fulfill either its promises of mercy or its threats of judgment.

We determine the quality of our lives and the nature of our destinies by our response to the Word of the Lord.

183

Who despises the day of small things?

(Zech. 4:10)

Scripture reading: Zech. 4:1-14

*T*he day of small things was the day a small group of people, survivors of the Exile, began to clear the rubble and rebuild the Temple.

Some onlookers were contemptuous of the project. They did not expect its completion, or they questioned its significance if completed.

In the power of the Spirit, however, the mountain of difficulty that loomed before the builders would be leveled. As sure as the foundation was laid the capstone would be set in place. People would hail the beginning and the completion of the task with shouts of praise.

Zerubbabel, chosen by God to lead the task of rebuilding the Temple, is given this prophetic message to encourage his heart and strengthen his hands. God is going to crown his labors with success.

Great things begin small. Small beginnings evoke the skeptic's scorn. But what faithful people undertake at God's command and for His glory will be accomplished. The mighty mountain will become level ground, and on that ground the Temple will arise. Trust God and get to work!

184

*When you fasted and mourned in the fifth and
seventh months for the past seventy years,
was it really for me that you fasted?
And when you were eating and drinking,
were you not just feasting for yourselves?
Are these not the words the Lord proclaimed
through the earlier prophets when Jerusalem
and its surrounding towns were at rest
and prosperous . . . ?*

(Zech. 7:5-7)

Scripture reading: Zech. 7:1-14

*D*uring the Exile, the Jews observed special days of
fasting each year. Now they have returned to their
homeland, and the Temple is being rebuilt. Should these
fasts be continued?

The Lord replies that fasting or feasting are vain unless the people suit intention to action. Their fasting and
feasting had been self-centered, not God-honoring. The
earlier prophets had condemned all fasts that were not ac-
companied by justice and mercy for oppressed and helpless people. Apart from righteousness, the fasting and
feasting were farces. Formal worship devoid of sincerity
had not prevented the Exile. Perpetuating such hypocrisy
would serve only to occasion new judgments.

Good activities can be spoiled by bad motives. True religion blends *what* we do and *why* we do it into whole-
hearted devotion to God.

185

It may seem marvelous to the remnant of this people at that time, but will it seem marvelous to me?

(Zech. 8:6)

Scripture reading: Zech. 8:1-13

What seems impossible to His people is possible to the Lord. We must not measure possibility by our wealth but by His "glorious riches" (Phil. 4:19).

The Lord promised to return to, and reside in, a rebuilt Jerusalem. Once again the city will teem with life. Old folks with walking sticks will thread their way through streets and squares filled with children at play.

Some returned exiles, looking at their small numbers and scant resources, labeled this an impossible dream. God says, "Not to Me!" "I will save my people . . . I will bring them back to live in Jerusalem . . . I will be faithful and righteous to them as their God" (vv. 7-8). The divine "I will" should quiet every human "We can't."

Possibility is not accurately measured by human efforts and human resources. It is measured by the purpose and the promise of the Almighty. He does not say, "Do what you can," but "Do what I tell you." Faith and obedience achieve the marvelous, the impossible.

186

"Was not Esau Jacob's brother?" the Lord says. "Yet I have loved Jacob, but Esau I have hated?

(Mal. 1:2-3)

Scripture reading: Mal. 1:1-5

*H*ate is used relatively and comparatively here, as it is in several scriptures. God favored Jacob over Esau by continuing the covenant with Abraham through Jacob's lineage and not Esau's.

God favored the Israelites over the Edomites by allowing the Israelites to return from exile and rebuild Jerusalem and the Temple, while former Edomite strongholds were permanently desolated.

All of this is related to the lives of the two nations in history, not to their destinies in eternity. The passage does not mean that all Israelites were chosen for heaven and all Edomites relegated to hell.

God is challenging Israel with the fact that superior privileges argue superior obligations. In light of all He had done for the house of Jacob, they are without excuse for any disloyalty to His covenant. Their sins will incur certain and severe judgment precisely because He has so loved and favored them.

"To whom much is given, of him will much be required" (Luke 12:48, RSV).

187

A son honors his father,
and a servant his master.
If I am a father, where is the honor due me?
If I am a master, where is the respect due me?

(Mal. 1:6)

Scripture reading: Mal. 1:6-14

*I*srael was God's son. The covenant commanded sons to honor earthly parents; how much more should the Heavenly Father be honored!

Instead, the very priests responsible for teaching the covenant despised God's name by colluding with the people to accept inferior offerings.

"When you bring blind animals for sacrifice, is that not wrong? When you sacrifice crippled or diseased animals, is that not wrong? . . . should I accept them from your hands?" (vv. 8, 13).

The Law required unblemished animals for sacrifices. The people were keeping the best and offering the worst. The priests were in cahoots with them, doubtless for a price.

God's name was profaned, and His altar was defiled. In holy anger He pronounces the guilty accursed!

God will not accept anything but the best from His people. That speaks powerfully to us and to our churches today!

188

Will a man rob God?

(Mal. 3:8)

Scripture reading: Mal. 3:6-12

God invites His people to return to Him, but this requires them to quit their sins. Here He specifies the heinous sin of robbery. He is the Victim of their thefts.

The accursed were aghast. "How do we rob you?" The answer was blunt, and denials were silenced: "In tithes and offerings" (v. 8).

The Law required the Israelites to bring a tithe of their "increase" to God. It was used to support the Temple and the priesthood.

The tithe was not a gift to God. It already belonged to Him. Not to bring it was to steal it. And in stealing from Him, they were robbing themselves, for He placed them under a curse, and their crops were failing.

God makes them a promise: "Bring the whole tithe into the storehouse," and I will "throw open the floodgates of heaven and pour out" uncontainable blessing upon you (v. 10).

Those who had argued, "I can't afford to tithe," were now learning that they couldn't afford not to tithe. God will not honor selfishness. When the selfish get rich they are being fattened for slaughter, as Scripture elsewhere teaches.

"The tithe . . . is the Lord's" (Lev. 27:30, KJV). Bring it and be blessed; steal it and be cursed.

Other Books by William McCumber

The Bible Speaks to Me About My Beliefs
BF083-411-285X

The God of New Beginnings
BF083-411-3651

Holiness Preachers and Preaching
(Great Holiness Classics, Vol. 5)
BF083-411-2892

Love Conquers All
BF083-411-4550

Matthew
(Beacon Bible Expositions, Vol. 1)
BF083-410-3125

Take a Bible Break
BF083-411-0806

The Widening Circle
BF083-410-8380

Order from your local bookstore, or call toll-free:

Beacon Hill Press of Kansas City
1-800-877-0700